D1615574

WE GO A-FISHING

The author playing a sea trout in the rock pool, Lærdal

WE GO A-FISHING

Francis Blaikie

Paul Harris Publishing

Edinburgh

First published 1975 by
PAUL HARRIS PUBLISHING,
50 Montrose Terrace, Edinburgh.

ISBN 0 904505 04 9.

Printed by The Shetland Times Ltd., Lerwick, Shetland.

CONTENTS

To June, my wife,
who married this fisherman, and who
does not seem to regret it — yet.

ILLUSTRATIONS

FOREWORD

The author has really written an autobiography of that part of his life which deals with fishing. He inherited a true love of this sport from his forefathers, who covered hundreds of years of Tweedside angling. Method used is, to him, the most important aspect of the sport, although he gives great detail of quantity of fish netted.

I have seen him catch and lose big and small fish, fall into the river, break his rod, and yet continue as if Kipling's *If* were his book of rules.

He does not burden the reader with too many technicalities, though fully qualified to do so, but offers us a share in the pleasure his rod has given him on numerous rivers and lochs in his lifetime.

Often, when fishing together, I have taken a rest on the opposite bank for the sheer pleasure of watching him in action. He gives the water careful scrutiny for the most likely spot for a fish, handles the rod superbly, casts gracefully with perfect control, and places the fly accurately. As he has grown older, he has become more selective and now uses nothing but fly, preferably dry-fly.

He is the perfect fisherman, enjoying everything to be seen on loch and river.

KNUT APOLD.

PREFACE

My father, the late Dr J. B. Blaikie, wrote a most delightful book forty-six years ago, called *I Go A-fishing*. His fund of stories was based on his diaries, which I have in my possession, and which I still enjoy reading. As a filial salute to the finest fly-fisherman I have ever seen in action, I have chosen the title for my own book accordingly, knowing full-well that I was a tenderfoot in such company. But one of the charms of fishing is that this great sport can be enjoyed quite independently of the technical prowess of the fisherman himself.

I think it is a great pity that more fishermen do not keep a record of their sport in the shape of a fishing diary: not just a list of catches made, but a description of their day: the weather, the height and condition of the water, their own and their friend's catch and the successful patterns of fly: any other items of interest such as falling-in, seeing a kingfisher or a red-necked phalarope (in different places, of course!), breaking a rod or even a contretemps with a bull! I have kept such a diary now for over forty years (only one bull), but I must own that it is not nearly so detailed as I would like it to be. My brother, Andrew, does it much better: an average of nearly a whole page per day.

However, I must honestly say that I can recollect practically every one of my 1000-odd days, just by reading about them. There is, though, one disgraceful train of entries in front of me as I write these words, covering four consecutive days in Norway 42 years ago:

Monday.	*Bright sun.*	*N.B.G.*
Tuesday	*ditto*	
Wednesday	*ditto*	
Thursday	*ditto*	

And as one ditto is as good as another, I have no recollection of what must have been desperately boring fishing. Candidly, I think with my present experience, these "dittos" could have been altered.

I have, for the greater part of my life, been a 'holiday' fisher, and there are many others who have had far greater angling experience. Furthermore, I have tended to go year after year to the same locality: I love returning to beautiful country I know. I like meeting all my friends again and, as the sum of enjoyment, in my view, is split between anticipation, fact and recollection, the first of these is so enhanced if you can visualise what you are anticipating. This thought is epitomised at the end of my chapter on Post-war Lærdal.

This book only covers fishing for salmon and trout and, generally speaking, "fly only." I used to spin years ago with an old-fashioned reel (a disastrous contraption, unless one had a reversible drum), but it bores me compared with the pleasure I derive from fly-fishing. What do I do when the river is high and dirty? I fish worm: much more fun — to me, at any rate.

Should any reader scan hopefully through the following pages for pearls of fishing wisdom and detailed instructions on how to be a proficient craftsman, he would be doomed to disappointment. This book is merely based on a browse through my diaries and, as my eyes roam over the pages, my memory is carried to the purples, blues and yellows of the Hebrides and Sutherland, or to the snow gently falling and disappearing into the ice-cold waters of the Don, or — best of all — to the crystal-clear flow of the Lærdal, where, as I write, I can see a large, grey-blue shape tilting upwards from the river's golden bed to suck down my dry-fly.

I am indebted to the editors of *The Field* and *The Flyfishers' Journal* for allowing me to include some of my articles published in those magazines: most of them are, so to speak, woven into the text.

I hasten also to thank my so-called 'editorial team!' This consists of four people: June, my wife; Andrew, my brother; Knut Apold and John Rintoul, fishing friends on so many of my holidays. As I completed each chapter, having read it to June (and amended it as instructed), it was then sent round the others, whose comments and suggestions have been invaluable. Knut was kind enough to offer to write a Foreword: my thanks to him for accomplishing this onerous task.

I have endeavoured to paint a picture of a number of fishing localities, including both their foregrounds and backgrounds, both serious and hilarious. The entries in my diaries remind me of all these episodes as though they had happened yesterday.

FRANCIS WILLIAM LANG BLAIKIE.

Ardentigh,
Rhu,
Dunbartonshire.
1975.

CHAPTER 1

FROM THE BURNS TO THE RIVERS AND LOCHS

For many hundreds of years, young (and possibly old) Blaikies have plopped their worms into the numerous burns of Roxburghshire and yanked half-pounders into the bracken, to be taken home and fried for supper. The Old Wood Burn meanders eastwards from the heights above Selkirk, through the gnarled remains of the ancient Ettrick Forest and towards the broad valley of the Tweed. The Eildon Hills, 'three crests against the saffron sky,' to the north: Rubers Law, dark and forbidding, to the south, and the placid hump of the Cheviot on the south-eastern horizon. Many's the time as a young boy I would delight in counting the brown and green fields as they stretched away from me to that mountain lying lazily some twenty-five miles away.

When I was very young, my sister, two brothers and I merely followed our ancestors who lived at nearby Holy-dean where the remains of the old castle wall and bake-house have stood for over four and a half centuries, and were taught how to catch these trout by our father who was born there. The line had to be as short as possible so that the differences of water depth and speed could be controlled. The pink worm was generally impaled on a No. 12 or No. 14 bait hook, but it was always important, according to my father, that no metal should be showing. A sinker was bitten on to the cast — some six inches above the bait — and the principal object was to ensure that your worm swam close to the bottom without hooking the stones, and, on the other hand, did not float on top of the water like a dry-fly.

But, curiously enough, we obtained our best sport in the tributaries of this burn. They were so small that one

had to bounce the worm through the grasses that grew
above them. Good trout were caught here, weighing up
to about ¾lb.

At that time of my life, around eight years of age,
I was actually keener on shooting. One fine September
evening my father allowed me to carry a rook-rifle down
the Old Wood Road (the Ancient Foss Way), and suddenly
he stopped and pointed with his eyes. About thirty yards
away, just to the right of a tree, a rabbit was sitting on
its haunches. I took careful aim and when the animal fell
over dead, my father was very excited: he had shot his
first rabbit in precisely the same spot over forty years
previously.

A little later on I was promoted to using a 12-bore
hammer-gun and we would walk up to the 'Helm' among
the bracken for the rabbits. There is no doubt that this
now obsolete weapon taught me the most important factor
in shooting, namely 'safety.' I am sure plenty today would
agree with me that there are still too many 'guns' whose
skill at killing game far surpasses that bedrock knowledge
of safety which, in my view, is the first lesson that should
be learnt.

I do not think that this exciting sport which I enjoyed
some fifty years ago made me into a good 'shot' (particularly in the air): it was 'snap-shooting' with a vengeance
and the greatest reward was to wait some seconds as the
rabbit coursed under the bracken out of sight, knowing
full well that forty yards away it had to leap over a disused wall into a wood. In that split second it was, at
least to a youngster, a great triumph to fire one barrel,
walk up to the wall and lift the rabbit lying dead on the
other side.

Our little burns were too small for fly-fishing, and
it was a number of years before we were taught how to
fly-cast. In the summer holidays of those days, our mother
took us year after year to Monreith in Wigtownshire and
my memory conjures up huge expanses of golden sand,

backed by deep caves, and a shrimping pool in which we slowly crept around, bare-legged, awaiting the thrill of an agitated shrimp or dab under our feet, to be transferred to a can filled with sea water and, later, cooked for tea.

Our first experience of loch fishing was enjoyed by us and numerous cousins at Faldonside Loch beyond Galashiels. It merely consisted of mounting a worm cast on some kind of rod, with a cork placed a foot up the from the bait, pitching the contraption into the water and awaiting that thrilling moment when the cork began to 'bobble,' then a few seconds more and you had your perch. Every time we made the trip a large number of fish were caught, but I cannot recollect if we ever ate any of the catch. As a matter of fact, I have since read that they are excellent for the table if skinned and properly prepared, but I am fairly certain they were never eaten in our day.

It was many years before I found the perfect location for burn fishing with the fly. I know full well that there are many thousands of burns and rivulets in these islands containing trout and almost every keen fisherman has his favourites, but mine happens to be in Arran, that beautiful mountainous isle jutting up between the western Mull of Kintyre and the Ayrshire coast to the east.

I used to visit this lovely island every year from 1933 until after the war. My mother-in-law owned a delightful bungalow at the foot of Glen Sannox — certainly one of the most beautiful glens in Scotland. I have fished the north and south burns for many years. The trout are very small due probably to lack of food, but they are possibly often very old and certainly very wary.

Fishing in the burns of Arran is, of course, a young man's sport and I would say that, ideally, the keen angler should be of an age between six and fifty. The water you fish is just deep enough for the fly, and if I could have arranged my sport's progress by a master plan rather than

B

by random opportunity, I should have gone to Arran twenty years earlier. The stooping, the crawling and the physical contortions which are a pleasure to the teenager become somewhat irksome to that terribly old fellow of around forty-plus.

The burns in Arran are miniature rivers. As I wade up in my sandshoes and creep beneath the overhanging alders, I am as a Giant in Lilliput. Multiply the scale tenfold, and it becomes the Spey or the Awe. These little rivulets are the small-scale model, just as the toy electric train you operate (instead of your son) is the real thing scaled down. But I must say this: the fish's range of vision is full-scale. It will see you two pools away in the clear, barytes-bearing water.

So the catching of fish (except, of course, in a spate) is one of the best angling exercises possible. You certainly cannot approach from upstream; the fish are under the stones long before you approach the pool.

Only by casting from below can you catch trout in normal fishing conditions. I am aware that upstream, nymph and/or wet-fly might do just as well — or even better. But I love watching that little olive dancing down the runs; first to the left, then waltzing to the right, and then hurrying down a stickle.

But the drag! That's what you fight all the time. Fish as short as you can and this curse can be minimised. Creep. Crawl. Mind the tree. Look out for the steep heather bank. There! A dimple and the lively eight-ounce fish plays very strongly on your hair-line cast.

You are miles from the burn's mouth. The water you fish is but a trickle — and still holds trout. The setting sun behind Cir Mhor rearing to westwards, casts golden beams of light down the valley. You lope homewards; looking out for adders underfoot, but you arrive back in the evening gloaming with six little fish to be fried in butter and eaten with crip oatcakes, followed by butter and honey and all washed down with good, strong tea. Then an icy dip in the sea (fifty yards away) before going to bed.

I would say that my experience in this lovely island with the dry-fly in the gin-clear water taught me more about fishing for difficult trout than anywhere else. My later experiences on such rivers as the Lærdal are mere extensions of these early lessons on the North and South Sannox where I learned to cast for those little fish in clear water, to gauge current swings and surges, keep out of sight and know instinctively where the trout would be undulating in the swim for their food — and all this among the wild heather and granite slopes with the fretwork of the darkening purple mountains set against the western sky.

At last came the great summer when we were allowed to spend an August fishing with our father. This is going back over forty years and it was at this time that I began to keep a fishing diary. We went to Ben Armine in Sutherland in 1927 and it was, apart from 1947, the driest August I personally have ever experienced. The midges were terrible; they actually at times drove us from the water. My sister, Jean, I recollect with horror, was one day wearing a puce jersey. In a flurry of slaps and curses I was fleeing from the river in an agony of midges and Jean was waiting for me. She was wearing a *grey* jersey, but it was in fact the same *puce* jersey, completely covered with millions of midges!

The river was reduced to a trickle. In fact, the fins of the salmon were sticking out of the water in the pools, but my father did quite well on dry-fly for the sea trout, having already fished the Lærdal for many years in the same fashion.

The Lodge was very comfortable and our mother looked after everything therein. I remember that — for some reason or another — I suffered a terrible nose-bleed. It was so bad that lying in my bed did not stop the flow, and in the morning my mattress was soaked in blood. I was worried. Not so my father; he said cheerfully that a little blood-letting was an excellent thing: the leech had gone a hundred years previously, but many people today could do with it.

We shot half the time — mainly walking-up grouse. I toiled many miles over the purple moors and in those days with a double-barrelled .410, I was a fair shot.

Andrew, my brother, and I 'had a go' at the river but, as far as I was concerned, not very successfully, except with the worm in the Round Pool. There was something terribly exciting about dropping a big lob worm into this pot, waiting a few minutes and then slowly pulling in. I had my first salmon there of 8½ lbs.

It was at Ben Armine that Andrew and I had our first, and probably last, experiment in poaching.

One day we decided to walk up the river to see whether there were any sizeable trout and soon after breakfast we were on our way, armed with 9-ft. rods, a worm dangling from each, to be dropped behind likely stones and in some of the deeper pools. I can still vividly remember the sun's power and the blinding glint on the water; the sudden lunge as the salmon and sea trout flashed to cover whenever we approached a pool; the croaking of the grouse in the heather, 'go-back, go-back, go-back'; the eagle which soared two hundred feet into the sky without as much as a flutter from its dark, outstretched wings. The hazy view: a sea of heather from horizon to horizon, from the massive bulk of Ben Klibreck rising steeply in the north-west to the twin crests of Ben Wyvis floating in the shimmering haze thirty miles to the southward. Heat . . heat . . everywhere. Swarms of clegs milling in the air and midge-clouds lilting to and fro' beside the limpid trickle flowing between the hot boulders forming the banks.

By the time we sat down and brought out our sandwiches, we had collected some twenty small fish. On more mature consideration, I should say the majority were smolts. Suddenly we noticed the head of what appeared to be a salmon protruding upstream from underneath a large rock in the middle of a pool. We immediately dropped our food and decided we should have 'cast about.' The only way to place the bait in front of the fish was to swing it on to the tip of the stone and gently agitate the rod until the worm fell off into the water — right in front of the large snout.

Having drawn lots, the game began. The first few casts were very clumsy, but soon we were able to present a wriggling worm to within one inch of the fish's slowly opening and closing mouth. After five minutes, we thought we had failed and this seemed certain when my hook became impaled, apparently on the underside of the rock. I strained the rod and suddenly a large grey shape swung into the stream, bringing my line with it, and, with an ecstatic yell, we realised that the salmon was 'on.'

The fish lunged up and down the small pool, always in full view, and Andrew replaced the net with a gaff head. The fight was uneventful: there was never any question of the fish leaving the pool as there was so little water. After ten minutes, Andrew crouched close to the water, gaff in hand, awaiting his cue. At last, the tiring fish wallowed past him; a quick stroke followed but the rusty gaff scraped the steel-blue back, fouled the line, and my rod sprang up — 'it's off!'

Baying like dogs, we fell to the ground and tore the heather out in handfuls; two boys cheated of their legitimate prize by a blunt gaff. Oh! Woe! Woe! For five minutes we sat moaning, almost in tears.

'Let's get it!' I truthfully cannot remember who made the suggestion, but there was neither argument nor discussion. Without further ado, we waded into the river and I took up a stance at the pool's narrow outlet with the net placed in the water between my legs, while Andrew plunged about in the water above, the unfortunate fish being chivvied from refuge to refuge until, in sheer desperation, it dashed downstream — right into my waiting net.

We splashed ashore and despatched it: 8 lbs. A very satisfactory and workmanlike job. All the way home we reassured ourselves that in all senses save in the technical, we had caught our fish in a fair and sportsmanlike manner. It was ours by right. The normal landing of the salmon had only been frustrated by a hundred-to-one chance — a blunt gaff. By the time we reached home, our mutual reassurances had assumed the form of a guilty man's defence in the dock and when we told the excited family of the wonderful fight, culminating in the brilliant gaffing, an abject feeling of depression and guilt had overtaken us. I often wonder whether our father ever suspected anything as our elation was entirely spurious and neither of us was a good actor.

At a distance of forty-eight years, I cannot help feeling that there must be a moral to this story. 'Don't poach and tell lies about it afterwards unless you're a good poacher and a better liar.' For our part, we might have qualified for the former but certainly not for the latter; we duly learned our lesson once and for all.

In August, 1928, the family went to the Owenmore in County Mayo: a lovely river flowing into the Atlantic opposite Achill Island. This river can still be classed as 'small' as no area of water is beyond the range even of your 9-ft. rod (which we used exclusively). I was beginning to recognise the likely places for salmon and sea trout, but I am always reminded of my father's remark at this time, that even the expert cannot locate a salmon 'lie' for a certainty when seeing a river for the first time. Of course, these are obvious at the faster heads and 'run-outs' of the pools, but very often there would be a hundred yards or so of slowly flowing glide in between and, without the knowledge of the topography of the river's bed, one needed a local expert (such as a gillie) to tell one, for instance, that there was a good salmon 'lie' just opposite that fence, half-way down.

It was here that I really and truly acquired the fishing

'bug' — never to recover — and all due to one day's fishing. There had been rain overnight, and the river was fining down to perfect fishing height. I went out by myself with my 9-ft. Forrest trout rod and one of those ungainly round nets which did not fold when not in use. (I am talking about forty-odd years ago). I was fishing for sea trout; thus a 2X cast, a No. 10 Butcher on the tail and a No. 12 Teal and Silver half-way up.

At the head of one pool I had a lovely, deep 'pull'; the fish slowly moved downstream and even then my meagre experience told me that this was a salmon. The fish played very well, possibly because I dared not put too much strain on it but soon it dawned upon me that the landing was going to present quite a problem. There were no shelving beaches, just steep banks straight down into the water. My net, in any case, was far too small but I had a gaff 'head' in my basket: how to exchange net for gaff? There was only one way. When at last the fish became quieter, I gripped the rod between my teeth and quickly unscrewed the net from its handle and substituted the small business-end of the gaff. All went well and I landed a small salmon of 5 lbs.

I was a very happy youth. Little did I realise, however, that I was to catch a further two grilse: the landing of these necessitated a reversal of the previous manoeuvre as I certainly did not want to gaff fish small enough to go into the net (3½ and 3¼ lbs.). So, once again, rod between teeth, remove gaff head, and replace net.

I certainly had beginner's luck that day; the thrill experienced is still with me.

During the following August, I had my first visit to Norway (q.v. the Evanger River) and in 1930, for a complete change, we went to the Isle of North Uist, of which I write in a separate chapter.

In 1931 we again returned to Ireland — the River Erne in County Fermanagh, a few miles upstream from Ballyshannon, at its mouth. This is a much larger river than any I had fished in Great Britain and salmon rods were used, except when indulging in the excellent trout-fishing. We stayed at Cliff House overlooking the river some fifty feet below at the bottom of the precipice. The owner, Major Moore (he would be dead by now), was 'wanted' by the Sinn Feinn in the 'Troubles,' and one day his pursuers entered by the front of the house, while he let himself down on a rope into the river at the back. He swam and scrambled his way to safety.

Nowadays, I am told, there is a hydro-electric dam on the river, but I have never returned to see its effect on the fishing. In 1931 there was an 'eel weir' just below the house, and on it a little brick building in the middle of the river where the Irish collected the eels as they swam upstream — still a very lucrative export.

The trout-fishing on the eel weir was fascinating: I wish I had had the experience that I enjoy now. In the evening (preferably a fine one), you would crawl along the stone weir in a crouching position and cast a dry-fly within inches of the side where the trout were waiting for flies dropping off the shaggy plants growing in the crevices.

I remember one day fishing a pool called 'Laputa' from a boat — Chisholm was 'gillieing.' I had just pulled in a lot of line and a grilse took my Teal and Silver close to the boat. The fish slowly ran downstream and my loose line followed. Imagine my horror when eventually I noticed it all clattering through the rod rings to disappear with a flop into the water. I had inadvertently burned it with my cigarette end.

We caught a number of salmon and quite a lot of fat trout up to about 2 lbs. weight. I spent one or two days on the other (left) bank of the river, fishing up the little runs under the overhanging trees with a Tup. As I was not yet twenty, this athletic type of fishing was fascinating and highly educational as there is no doubt that such sport teaches the young enthusiast much more than days spent in a boat. How to cast to avoid the 'drag' where the trout will lie: how to fish and cast to avoid the over-hanging branches: how and when to strike: how to wade on slippery stones without falling in. I think it took me longer to master the last lesson than any other — the one golden rule (bitter experience has taught me this) is *never* to move a foot until the other is secure on a firm base.

I have, in the past few years, fished on two small rivers which are very similar, although some two hundred miles apart: the River Ruel in Argyllshire and the Snizort in the Isle of Skye. I have visited the former on a number of occasions and have stayed at the most excellent hotel at Ormidale, owned by Mr and Mrs Chance. Alas! It no longer exists as one. The river is very small and requires plenty of water to bring it into 'ply': it winds its way down among the bracken-clad banks to Loch Ridden.

I only caught it 'right' once. I had a few days' holiday there, during which the river was down to a trickle. There were quite a lot of salmon and sea trout in the pools, but they would accept no fly, dry or wet, in the daytime nor at night. However, at the end of my stay, we had a good day's rain, and I immediately hooked and landed a 7 lb. salmon on my 9-ft. trout rod. No sooner had I restarted to fish than I hooked another: my wrist was so sore playing the first fish that I murmured, 'Oh, Lord!' I was extremely thankful that the Deity immediately heard my prayer and unhooked the salmon. That day I had two fish weighing 15¼ lbs. and a sea trout.

The Snizort winds northwards for miles over the moors in Skye, and we stayed at the Skeabost Hotel near its north. Like the Ruel, this small river needs plenty of water to bring it into good fishing 'ply.'

Rather an amusing episode happened one day as I was fishing down the right bank while my friend, Bill Gibbs, cast from the opposite side.

We came to a pool with a narrow neck and Bill

had the first cast down (he was only a few yards across the river), but he had no luck. When he had reached the bottom of the pool, I had a cast myself at its head (a single size 10 'Jock,' 6 lb. B.S. cast mounted on my 9-ft. trout rod). I took a step forward and cast — crash! My rubber waders slipped on the wet rock and I went flat on my face. My rod shot from my hand and I, just in time, rescued it from the deep water. Luckily my personal damage only amounted to a slightly-cut nose, so I staggered up and lifted the rod — there was a salmon on. It weighed 6½ lbs. One is very lucky sometimes.

I used to love to walk upstream for at least four miles and fish down, practically every cast presenting a fresh problem: water-speed and depth always altering; its direction ever-changing, one's skill being tested to the full in the art of river wet-fly fishing.

While thinking of small rivers, I recollect with great pleasure the few occasions I have fished the chalk streams in Southern England: particularly do I remember the Itchen in Hampshire. Through the kindness of the late Tommy Phelps at Kingfisher Lodge, Brambridge, I used to fish the odd day on this delightful stream. What a far cry from the wildness of the Highlands and the grandeur of Norway! 'Lush, green meadows' might be an over-worked phrase when describing this countryside, but no words can better describe the peace of the chalk stream; and the cows, standing up to their knees in buttercups, dreamily staring into space. The only thing which is sur-prising to me, common to the Itchen and the Highland loch, is the ubiquitous sand-piper. It is so incongruous to hear its 'peep-peep' as it darts up and down close to the limpid water. There used to be a barn owl which hunted by day, turning in the air and swooping up and down in utter silence.

I only once really caught the 'duffer's fortnight.' One early June evening, I left the Lodge and sauntered up-stream. Above the Water Works I came to a longish pool where a few good trout were sucking down newly-hatched Mayflies. Those who have experienced a really good rise, such as this, will agree it is often very simple. I merely took each trout in turn from the foot of the pool, taking care to bring the hooked fish downstream so as not to disturb the rest. In the hour, at this one pool, I landed seven weighing 16 lbs., the best 3.3. I also had three grayling amounting to 4.13, the best 2.7.

Chalk streams are seldom as easy as this. There is no doubt that a greater knowledge of entymology than I possess is required and the fish are generally much more 'choosey' than their north-country cousins.

Furthermore, at times I had exceptional difficulty in hooking the grayling as they came straight up from the bottom and whether I struck quickly or slowly, it was often the same result — no fish. I, once or twice, had a good day for grayling on the Test at Stockbridge in December with three small wet flies fished across the stream. Unfortunately, quite often I would hook a two or three-pound brown trout to be carefully returned to the water: an ugly, eel-like brute in shocking condition.

For a few years after the last war I lived near Berkhamsted in Hertfordshire, and I had a day or two on the River Glade nearby. I caught some trout, but I am always reminded of a horrible piece of showmanship on my part.

It was on a Saturday and I had cast from the main road bridge, a couple of miles north of Hemel Hempstead. I was fishing dry and, to my consternation, I immediately attracted a crowd of ten or twenty spectators (I doubt if any of them were fishers).

"This is all very easy," I ventured, chancing my arm. "Just cast your fly and land your fish." So I cast and, to my surprise, hooked a pound trout: gasps of wonder and incredulity from the audience around me. I was on top of the bridge so I, so to speak, put all my winnings on a possible 'grand coup.'

"Now, ladies and gentlemen, it is quite easy to land a fish in these circumstances without a net — which you couldn't use anyway. Just play the trout 'dead' (which I did), slowly draw it in, like so (which I did), and then, without jerk or fuss, sweep it up on to the bridge," (which I did). I knocked the trout on the head and donated it with regal magnaminity to a beautiful blonde standing beside me. I flashed a benign smile to the awe-struck crowd and walked slowly away, humming a little tune at my disgusting smugness.

And now I come to the bigger rivers — the Spey and the Awe. Keith and Margaret Walker have a delightful house a couple of miles up the River Avon, a tempestuous tributary of the Spey. June and I have been there half-a-dozen times or so since the war as their guests —and how we look forward to these weekends. The combination of lovely surroundings, Margaret's delicious picnics of her own garlic pâté and, sometimes, superb fishing, is the perfect prescription for pleasure.

One year, we would go up at Easter and the next at the end of May or the beginning of June. The Easter trips are not generally very successful from the fishing point of view, as I do not, as a rule, spin, and in March or April, the conditions are Arctic and generally unsuitable for fly-fishing.

However, one Eastertide at the end of March, 1964, I had uncommon luck. It was beastly cold and Keith, Margaret and I were fishing Tulchan D. My host and hostess were, of course, spinning in the icy water, while I went away and played with a salmon fly. The patterns I was using were three-inch monstrosities which I had inherited from my father and they had probably never been in the water for at least thirty-odd years. They were all tatty and bedraggled, but they did have iron eyes. All the feathers had split into their individual fibres, and it was difficult to nominate their species except by the faded body. They were heavy and clumsy and must have swum

well, their pliant hackles and wings waving in the current
(à la modern tube flies?).

In the four days of fishing, I caught a few kelts,
plus a fresh fish every day, one, incidentally, being a
baggot). Keith and Margaret, I think, actually take pride
in the fact that, during the same time, they landed one
fresh fish between them.

Why was this? I do not have the experience on fishing
on the Spey in March and April to know whether this
adventure constituted a four-day wonder, or whether, perhaps, in certain particular conditions of river, temperature
and barometer, the fish will indeed prefer swimming hackles
to spinning hardware. No doubt Keith has given the fly
its chance in the Easters since then, but, up to date, I
have not heard.

By the end of May onwards, the method of salmon
fishing has completely changed. Small Hairy Marys and
Blue Charms are delicately cast with floating lines. The
lush and beautiful Spey valley is spread out round you,
and the fishing hut is covered with a mass of fragrant
honeysuckle.

Keith is an expert on the so-called 'greased-line'
method. He holds a length of loose line in his left hand,
and when he sees the salmon roll over his fly and turn
away, it is allowed to run through his fingers until the
tightening comes. I am not good at this technique; having
fished possibly eighty per cent of my time for trout. I find,
when the time comes, instinct compels me to strike, even
if very slowly. Not that I do not catch fish this way
(I believe there are those who consider that one *should*
strike without loose line), but Keith's self-discipline is a
delight to watch, and highly efficient in practice.

One year he kindly offered me, as a sub-let, a week
on the Kincardine water near Nethy Bridge. It was a
glorious hot spell, and I actually rose, in those six days
of fishing, twelve salmon to my low-water patterns, but
only landed two. If I had had the experience Keith has

in such circumstances, I should surely have landed a larger proportion.

I have probably only fished on a couple of dozen days altogether on the Spey. There are those, of course, who ply it day after day throughout the whole fishing season for years on end. My knowledge of it is, therefore, really very meagre, but it is enough to convince me that this beautiful river has everything a good salmon water should have: delightful surroundings, fascinating sport, and very charming people — surely the three 'musts' for an angler's heaven.

I have only fished the Awe on a few occasions, through the kindness of the late Jimmie Woodrow, in the month of September. Knut Apold and I made these trips together. When I think of bad wading, my mind turns to North Uist (q.v.), the Castle Pool on the Teith, and the Awe. The weed is abundant, and I attribute the fact that I have not *yet* fallen in, to Divine Providence.

A few years ago I had a most enjoyable day. Fishing with low-water pattern flies, I had three small salmon before lunch. Unfortunately, afterwards my salmon rod broke at a ferrule when casting so that was my fishing over.

On the following year again, the bed of the river was paved with salmon and grilse. Fishing this time with a No. 8 Hairy Mary and a white floating line on my 9-ft. 6in. Lærdal rod, I actually rose eight: two didn't touch, four were just 'on and off,' and I landed two fresh grilse of 6 and 5¼ lbs. Jimmie had a couple of nice salmon, and Knut one.

A lovely day on a beautiful river with charming companions: perhaps a little more skill on my part in hooking the fish: whether to retain a yard of loose line or to strike with a tight line. My Spey experience all over again! I feel that probably the 'loose line' method is the correct one, but I am afraid I am probably too lazy to follow it.

I have devoted a large part of my subsequent chapters

on North Uist and Kinlochbervie to loch fishing in these districts. However, I have also spent many pleasant days on other sheets of water in England and Scotland, generally after brown trout. Although preferring to cast from the shore, I have generally used a boat — particularly in the larger lochs, and I have so often been surprised by the almost universal habit of so many of my companions who, although otherwise experienced and successful anglers, seem almost invariably to cast continuously down-wind. As a rule, of course, the boat is drifting in this direction and my companion has often been an adept entomologist and is an expert at choosing the most successful team and size of flies. He fishes at different depths and speeds and, as often as not, catches as many fish as I do. I have, however, always considered it of the utmost importance that the angle of casting should ever be changing. On some days, and at certain times, the fish seem to prefer a team of flies retrieved directly against the wind: on others, they rise much better if the lures are pulled across the wave or at some angle between parallel with, and at right angles to, the boat. There are even times when it is worth trying the odd cast sideways to the breeze and dragging the dropper *with* the wind. This is particularly effective when nearing the leeward end of the loch where, so often, the trout are stationed with their tails practically touching the shore, awaiting their food as it drifts down to them. This fact is also worth remembering when fishing the leeward shore from the bank.

In 1956 on the famous Chew Valley Lake near Bristol, brother Andrew and I had a very welcome invitation to have a cast from the shore; this was a year before it was opened to the public. I remember we were rather crestfallen on being told that we could retain a maximum of three trout each, but this instruction was immediately softened by being told that no fish under two pounds was to be kept! Fishing with two flies only (No. 10 Dunkeld on the tail), I hooked a beauty close to the shore, which

played like a sea trout, and, when landed, weighed 4 lbs.
9 ozs. Directly I saw its beautiful shape and complete
absence of any red spots, I realised the truth that, in
fact, the brown and sea trout are the same fish.

Later I caught another of 3 lbs. 3 ozs., and then
had a terrific fight with a 'rainbow,' which took me over
five minutes to land, but it had to be returned as it weighed
only about 1¾ lbs.

Andrew had less luck, but possibly more exciting
sport. He was wading out on a long rocky promontory
and hooked a monster. It played in a very sedate manner,
boring slowly and deeply around him, but taking out little
or no line. This tug-of-war lasted some ten minutes; then
the fish suddenly decided that the game had lasted long
enough and it applied increasing pressure, moving slowly
out into the lake. Andrew's line disappeared, and his
backing followed out and out until, after a few minutes,
it had all gone and the inevitable break occurred. How
big? The fish never showed, but Andrew was quite certain
it was in the five to ten pound bracket.

In 1949, June, Andrew, John Rintoul and I spent
an August fortnight in Lewis. The sun beat down on us
relentlessly the whole time, and I have never in my
life been so overcome with the heat and general lassitude
it engenders. Loch Valtos is generally excellent salmon
water, but conditions were so against fishing that our results
were very poor, except the odd trout in some of the other
lochs which took a dry-fly on the glassy calm.

One evening, however, stands out vividly in my
memory. We were trying to catch brown trout on Valtos
in the gloaming; it was dead calm. Wet and dry were tried
with little success.

Even at midnight there was still an eerie northern
light in the sky and, suddenly, at about 1 a.m., we heard
a cuckoo miles away. The noise slowly approached from
the distant Harris hills to the south, and we could, at last,
discern the bird flying north across the flat, calm loch,

'cuckoo-ing' all the time. It disappeared into the gloaming, its call growing fainter and fainter until the night was hushed to stillness.

Some minutes later we suddenly noticed a pale grey van careering at breakneck speed along the Stornoway road. It seemed to glide over the ground; not a sound could we hear, although it was only a hundred yards away. With a peculiar feeling of unreality, we watched this apparition pass us and then as noiselessly vanish into the night. We thereupon decided that the fishing was no good anyway and pulled the boat to its moorings as the first grey light of dawn flushed the eastern sky beyond the dark wilderness of moor and loch.

In Ardgour there is a delightful loch called Doilet, and I have fished it on a number of occasions with my late friend, Teddy Deane. We used to stay the night in Strontian and take the road over the pass. Doilet is clad with dense fir trees and you might just as well be in the wilds of Canada as in Western Scotland. We used to hear the stags roaring all around us in the mountains.

Upon reflection, I think we should have made our visits earlier in the year. In September the salmon are already smoked! However, we caught quite a number of large sea trout and I remember, on one occasion, during a dead calm, mentioning to Teddy that one could occasionally catch fish on such unpropitious occasions by casting a long line, letting it sink, and then slowly drawing it towards you in a series of jerks. I actually hooked two salmon and a sea trout within the next half-hour by this method, but, unfortunately, they all came unstuck. My 'candid camera' snapshot of Teddy was taken during one of these calms on the loch.

And so I come to say a few words at last about Loch Lomond. As so much has been written about the charms and the fishing on Loch Lomond by eminent authors, I am only going to give it a passing word, although I used to visit it on very many occasions. I have always said that

C

it is the most beautiful loch on which to catch nothing! This is a little unfair, but precise knowledge of the sea trout's habitat ('an oar's depth') is vital. I love fishing round the islands between Luss and Balmaha, and often is the time I have landed on the sandy beach of Inchmoan and cooked a steak for lunch on a wood fire, with my late friend, Willie Simons.

The sea trout are of a good size (though my best is but 6½ lbs.), and the 'blacknebs' (= herling, = whitling, = 'grilse sea-trout') are one of the fastest growing breeds in the British Isles.

Once or twice I have been out with Ronald Strang who has a boat up at Ardlui. We used to row over on a May or June day to the eastern bank where the trees hang over the water from the rocks above. Great sport was enjoyed with the brown trout waiting for the insects falling on to the water from above; and the fish are of a good size.

The River Fruin runs eastwards into the loch down the glen of that name, and it is purely a spate river. If it is too high and dirty, it is no good with the fly. It must be falling and 'port-wine' coloured: such ideal conditions only last for a few hours and then the water is too low. I used to spend hours on a sunny September day crawling up the banks with a dry-fly or a nymph, but I do not recollect getting as much as a rise from a sea trout, although there is the occasional good brownie. I have since been told that the sea trout return to the loch with the falling river until, of course, in late October and November they begin to think about spawning.

CHAPTER 2

RIVER DON

The Don was really my 'school' as far as fishing was concerned. I have visited it on eighteen Eastertides, and I went to it first with my father in 1927. Always in those days we stayed at the Forbes Arms Hotel, Bridge of Alford, and either fished the hotel water or rented a private beat (generally Lower Brux). I had ample opportunity to watch my father's skill and to derive a fund of education as to trout fishing: how to cast wet-fly, dry-fly, including a combination of the two, namely, 'dibbling' (more about this later). I learnt not only how to cast in any direction and under any conditions, but also *where* to cast.

I would like to say a few words about my father, knowing full-well that I was too near him to make a balanced judgment. He was born near Bowden, close to the River Tweed, and his forebears were all Tweedside men and women, stretching back for at least six centuries. The Blaikies have always been farmers; my great-great-grandfather rode from Bowden to London and back to meet Farmer George at the beginning of the nineteenth century, and I have a copy of the diary he wrote, in which he describes meeting the King, who "spoke good broad English, and distinct, yet repeating so fast one is apt to lose him in part." His brother, my great-great-grand-uncle, Francis Blaikie (after whom I was named) was factor to the famous Coke of Norfolk, the first Earl of Leicester. Francis spent most of his life at Holkham, and his portrait still hangs in the estate office there.

My father was, therefore, a countryman, born and bred; and yet he saw fit, after studying medicine at Edinburgh, Heidelberg and Freiburg Universities, to set off to London and become a town-dweller. I feel he eventually enjoyed his life in the capital, but mainly because of his in-born interest in human beings and his skill as a medical practitioner, which tested his attributes to the full. There is no doubt, however, that he often hankered after his native land — particularly for the burns and rivers of his childhood.

He was particularly at ease with the very old and very young and especially the latter. He adored children, and used to enthral his juvenile patients with his skilful imitations of the call of owls, pigeons, curlews, and many wild animals. I recollect one episode which was so typical of him.

A young and very ill boy was convalescing after a serious operation. My father visited him one day to find him much improved and looking at a stamp collection. Now, my father had (which I have now) a collection I would describe as a fair schoolboy's some eighty years ago. So my father asked the lad about the stamps he saw in front of him, as even he could see that they were of considerable value.

"Swops at school: would you like to have them, sir?"

"Thank you very much, my lad," said my father, not batting an eyelid, but with a twinkle in his eye. The boy, somewhat crestfallen, handed over his album.

That night a visit had already been arranged to another patient, Michael Stephens, who owned possibly the finest stamp collection in the Kingdom outside the royal one.

"Michael," said my father, "these look pretty good to me and actually belong to an eight-year-old lad who's been very ill. What are they worth?"

Stephens examined them for a few minutes and then "I'll give you three hundred pounds!" (This about 1925, by the way!).

It gave my father so much pleasure next day to hand over the fat cheque, and he said that the way the boy's face lit up did both the patient and the doctor a power of good.

And why was he such a wonderful fisherman? Although he was my father, I still persist in believing he was the finest fly-angler I have ever known. This, I feel, was basically due to his intimate knowledge of nature. When he went fishing, he knew not only what he saw, but what to look for. He always used to tell us about the various animals and birds he had seen during the day, while I, poor London-bred son that I am, saw but a fraction (I am improving in old age).

This feeling for nature, in his blood for hundreds of years, made him a natural fisherman. He was inexorable in his pursuit of the fish; his 'fly on the water, and his eye on the fly.' He became part of his surroundings. He was at one with the river and the trees and the fields and the hills, and his inborn knowledge seemed to include the fishes beneath the surface of the burn, river or loch.

Apart from all this, his casting was a glorious sight to behold, whether on a small river or on the Lærdal. No strain; just a delicate throw, shooting out to the spot where — almost always — a fish was waiting for his fly.

His great 'tip' on casting a fly is now fairly well-known but it is invaluable. Once it is mastered, it is really only a matter of time and practice to become proficient at the art. "Always consider the level of the water to be two or three feet higher than it really is." In this way the fly will land softly on the surface, and, furthermore, it is a 'must' if you are 'shooting' your line to gain more distance.

I have also evolved a 'tip' of my own, albeit a somewhat bizarre one to anyone who might be watching me. All fishermen, on numerous occasions in their fishing experience, will become hooked up in some tree behind them. One day on the Don I had become involved in no less than four trees: they were some twenty yards behind me and my language became somewhat more scarlet every time I became hung up. Then I had what I thought was a brilliant idea. I turned my back on the river and cast towards a three or four foot gap between the trees, the following back cast alighting on the river. This is now almost my invariable habit when trout-fishing with a line of trees immediately behind me but, as I say, to an on-looker I must be 'nuts.'

The unselfishness which ruled my father's life was never more apparent than in his sport. I was lucky enough to know a great friend of his, Harry Plunket Greene, who was the author of my favourite fishing book, *Where the Bright Waters Meet*. My father died during his presidency of the Flyfishers' Club and Plunket Greene took over from him. Alas! He, himself, died soon afterwards; not, however, before writing an obituary of my father which contained the following words:

> " . . . there was nothing he would not do, fair or foul, to manoeuvre his partner into the best places . . . .".

No fisherman could wish for a finer epitaph.

My general impression, looking back over forty years on the Don, is one of snow and the all-pervading cold. However, such was the quality of the trout fishing, one seldom minded the weather conditions, and quite often there would be a furious hatch of March Browns or Olives in a thick blanket of snowflakes drifting down from the grey sky. The hotel guests would glance out of the window in the morning at the maelstrom outside, saying "Not for ME, today! " And yet some — particularly my father — would brave the elements and bring back nine or twelve pounds of trout. In actual fact, of course, the air temperature rises when it snows.

We used to fish the wet-fly until the rise came on, then change to dry Baigent flies — magnificent floaters that they were, and are. The colder the day, the later the rise. If it is warm and balmy (which it seldom is in April!), regiments of flickering flies float down about mid-day. If very cold, it can be three o'clock before the real fun starts — if then.

I remember so vividly the half-hours my father and I used to spend waiting for the car at Bithnie Bridge on Lower Brux. This wooden span, since replaced by a Bailey Bridge, is close underneath the road, a mile west of Bridge of Alford. Below it is a nice-looking salmon pool, curling round to the right, slowing to perfect dry-fly water for trout when the rise is on.

We would have finished our day at about 5 p.m., the cold morning possibly yielding a brace of trout to the wet-fly. About mid-day you would discern a few March Browns or Olives beginning to flutter downstream, and hurriedly the reel was changed to one with a floating line and a Baigent dry-fly. A dimple here and there, and if you placed it just right, it would disappear in a quiet swirl . . . then away! The Don trout play magnificently, and maybe in a few minutes you would have one of $\frac{3}{4}$, or 1, or $1\frac{1}{2}$, or 2 lbs., or even bigger, in your net.

By this time, the armies of flies glided past you in their thousands. The splashes of rising trout covered the water's surface, and you had to try and keep calm and choose your prey.

You cast again — you missed him. You shortened line and had a go at a good fish within six feet of you. You hooked him, and, after a wonderful fight, you landed your two-and-a-half pounder.

And so it went on; for twenty minutes or half-an-hour. Then the flies thinned out; the rises were fewer and in five minutes the river's surface was devoid of fly or rise. You then took a few quick bites at your sandwich and a swig of beer or hot soup (probably 2 p.m. by now), keeping a sharp look-out at the same time.

During the afternoon you could, if lucky, pick up the odd fish, but by 5 p.m., the sport had finished (it often came on again around 6 o'clock).

And so I met my father at Bithnie Bridge. He would have possibly twelve pounds of trout: myself, if lucky

(and proud of it) around eight pounds. He would then
change his cast to IX, mount a little low-water Lady
Caroline on to it, and throw it with a gentle 'plop' to
the far side of the incoming stream, just below the bridge,
the line being 'mended' as the incredibly unlikely-looking
fly (it was my father's favourite) swam down and across.
Just as it was snatched into the current, a blue-grey back
would slither over to it, the rod top would be dropped
and then raised again — the fish was 'on!' Then ten
minutes of fun and I would gaff a fresh nine-pounder
lower down in the pool. By this time, it would be 5.30,
and the car waiting for us above. Incidentally, in six
consecutive days of 'final casts' for salmon at Bithnie,
my father one year had five salmon.

Then we swept back to the Forbes Arms for a cup
of tea in front of a roaring fire amid a hubbub of conversation as we all exchanged our day's stories.

The following is a word-for-word quotation from my
father's diary, dated 25th April, 1932. Unfortunately, I
was not there to see the fun, but brother Andrew was:

"Snow storms. Got a fish Lower Forester 2 lbs.
and lost a much bigger one: plus three small. At
end of day at Bithnie hooked, on my Lennox rod
and small, double-hooked Dusty Miller, a fish that
played splendidly. Took me right down — after first
threatening to go through the far side of the bridge—
to below the farm. A. tried to gaff it before then,
but when it saw him, it ran straight across the river.
A. supported me whilst I struggled down the river
outside the bushes. When I got it near him, it again
dashed off and A. fell on his back in the water.
Further down, A. skilfully gaffed it when about ten
yards from the bank. It struggled, he stumbled, and
it got off the gaff. But luckily the hook held and
he managed, a little later, to gaff it again and bring
it to the bank. A lovely cock fish of 21½ lbs."

What a wonderful fight it must have been!

Sunday fishing was rather fun. As an acknowledgment of the Day, we never wore waders, never took a basket, and only cast for fish we had seen rise! In other words, we sauntered out of the hotel if it were fine (which it so often is on Sundays) in our best tweed suits and shiny brown shoes, a sandwich in our pockets and a rod in our hands — dry-fly only. This sort of self-absolution always used to make us smile.

I remember particularly one day; it was glorious. High billowy white clouds sped across the blue sky, the hot sun blinking in and out. The peewits turned and swooped, screeching over the rich, brown furrows. Dippers darted above the water's surface, alighted on a stone and gave us a couple of curtsies; and, as usual, the lambs were always losing their mothers.

My father and I sat down on the green sward, a few hundred yards downstream of the hotel, at a pool aptly named 'The Aquarium.' We smoked our pipes and watched . . . and waited . . . .

Suddenly there was a dimple right under the far bank: without a word, my father lifted his rod and twenty-five yards of line curled out across the river, the fuzzy Baigent alighting just right: two feet above the rise . . . . a swirl . . . .

And so it went on. A cast now and again (there was no concentrated rise that day), and, at tea-time, and slightly guiltily, we walked back to the hotel with thirteen trout weighing fourteen pounds — a lovely basket.

Nowadays, I generally stick to dry-fly, unless there is no rise at all. Possibly I may not catch so many fish, but the size seems to be better. This is probably due to the fact that, when a natural rise is spotted, the good fish can be picked out. If the correct artificial is placed just above a rising trout, and it is, so to speak, 'floating on tip-toes,' then a rise is a near certainty.

It so happens that my best day ever on the Don occurred quite recently. Miss Chetwynd of Fetternear very kindly gave me a couple of days, and it was one of these times when conditions were just right.

The first was coldish, but no wind, snow nor rain. There was no hectic rise lasting half-an-hour: just an odd fish rising here and there all day. I started with a March Brown nymph on the tail, and a Baigent Brown half-way up the cast. I immediately caught a fish on the nymph, but eventually the floating fly seemed the more attractive, so I, thereupon, fished with two Baigents! I finished at 4.30 p.m. with seventeen fish weighing 16.2 lbs. The best (2 lbs.) I first thought was a smolt as I noticed the little dimple: the bigger the fish, quite often, the smaller the rise.

The next day, however, was not so happy. For once, I started fishing wet, and then the flies began to come down. I changed my reel, took the mounted dry-fly off my hat; there was a gust of wind, and the whole contraption was swept out of my grasp and went floating away down the river. Muttering darkly, I prepared a replacement while the flop-dollopers were cavorting all round me. When eventually ready, I caught three trout in quick succession — all to be returned! The Don fish play so well, even a six-ounce fish will take you perhaps a couple of minutes to the net. Then I spent another valuable two minutes each time unravelling the ghastly mess in my cast. Meanwhile, the rises grew less and less, and I was in a state of moaning near-collapse.

However, the Fates were fairly kind to me in that I had 8 = 7 lbs. up to 2 lbs., and I had to tear myself away from Avenue Pool at 3 p.m. when the rise was still 'on' to drive back to Glasgow.

I caught my first salmon ever on the fly on the Don in 1928. I was fishing 'wet' for trout in the Upper Forester Pool (Lower Brux) with the same team as usual: March Brown on tail, Professor Cash and Greenwell — all size 12. The salmon really seem to like the small March Brown:

this eight-pounder gave me a great thrill on a 9ft. rod and 2X cast.

I mentioned 'dibbling' (or 'dibbing' as some have it) earlier in this chapter. This can be a most killing method when the water is high and dirty and the fish are sheltering from the strong main stream at the comparative slack at the sides of the river. My father used to do great execution, while others fishing in such conditions in the orthodox manner, often caught nothing at all. On the tail we tied a March Brown of a rather bigger size than usual — probably 8 or 10. This, so to speak, acted as an anchor. Very near the top of the cast you had your stiff-hackled Baigent Brown; the flies were then thrown into the turgid, coloured stream on a short line (4 or 5 yards), and, as they swung out of the current, the rod-top was raised and the Baigent 'dibbled' round on the water's surface.

I remember I was once fishing 'Paradise' (and it is 'Paradise'!) on the Monymusk beat when conditions were just right for 'dibbling,' and I rose a very good trout on the Baigent as it realistically hopped round on the surface. It was just 'on and off.' I cast again. To my astonishment, the fish rose again . . . . dammit! Off again! A third similar thing happened next cast, and on the fourth I hooked the trout firmly on the March Brown — a lovely one of 2 lbs. 6 ozs. Why the fish was not pricked, I shall never understand; it could only be that, in each case, the point of the hook must luckily have been outside the fish's mouth.

I wonder how many fishermen will appreciate and condone the following episode, or merely dismiss it as a symptom of youthful lunacy? When I was about 18, I was casting up-stream against half a gale, and I was in a furious temper. The wind was so bad that the fly was often swept back to hook itself on my clothing; on one occasion, I removed it from my cheek!

After half-an-hour of this, I worked myself up into

a terrible tantrum. With an extra-special effort, I whipped
the cast into the teeth of the gale — crack! my cast
was gone. But I was not dismayed — oh, no! I actually
went on casting with a bare line for five minutes, just to
show the elements I didn't care. Silly and childish, but
I know there will be readers who have been in a similar
situation and will understand.

Charlie (long since dead, alas) and Mary Spence used
to do us proud at the Forbes Arms. The food was quite
excellent: breakfasts of porridge and large glass jugs of
cream, fried trout and bacon and eggs lying in their serried
ranks in front of a roaring fire. Then home-made oatcakes
and local heather honey. When the weather was inclement
on a Sunday and we couldn't sally forth, we would have
for lunch a plate of tender, underdone cold roast Angus
beef off the bone with pickled walnuts for piquancy. My
mouth waters at the memory.

We always slept in the hotel annexe — a hundred
yards down the river from the hotel: many's the evening
we used to pick up a nice trout from the garden on the
way over to change for dinner. No central heating (at
least, not in those days), and the ice-cold sheets as you
climbed warily into bed caught your breath until your
feet found the large, stone hot-water bottle. (As far as
I was concerned, there was always an almighty crash sometime during the night as it tumbled to the floor!)

The Don, in my view, and in my comparatively limited
experience, is the perfect trout river for novice and expert
alike. Beautiful water of infinite variety in idyllic surroundings, and always the chance of a salmon on your
trout rod. I unhesitatingly recommend any keen fisherman
to go there in late March, April or May. It can be
desperately cold. The snow-storms can swirl round you all
day; you may feel miserable but my rose-coloured memory
convinces that the Don is the trout river for me.

Chapter 3

ISLE OF NORTH UIST

North Uist! Halcyon days of brilliant sunshine on the machair. Broad sweeps of deep, turquoise sea to the delicate, pale sands stretching out into the Atlantic. St. Kilda but beads of mercury on the hard horizon. The larks fluttering skywards, their insistent song for ever in your ears. The up-ended swans on Loch Hosta and the mallard family forging across the ripple. An island of colour from the distant smudge of Ben More in South Uist to the Harris hills in the north: a carpet of blue lochs set in purple heather and brown peat hags, and that feeling of silent peace and contentment and loneliness and space . . . All this is what North Uist means to me.

I went there first with my father and the family in 1928. We stayed at Newton Lodge, since become a hotel. We spent most of our time fishing, shot now and again (grouse, golden plover — shame! — duck, and a stag). We even waded across to the Isle of Lingay at the neap tide and gaffed out over 20 lbs. of lobsters from underneath the rocks. We had a surfeit of them for supper that night. My father told me later it was his opinion that there was something definitely inebriating about lobsters. Apparently everybody was shouting at the top of their happy voices afterwards — *without* the aid of any alcohol!

My father's friend, the late Sir Harold Graham-Hodgson, who later became radiologist to the King, came with us. One Sunday morning we sauntered down to the shore nearby to a reputed ancient broch to see if we could find some old coins or pieces of native glass. Somebody suddenly picked up a queer-looking bone: what was it? We asked G.-H., the expert. He didn't know, but was extremely interested. He had forgotten most of the facts regarding pre-historic animals: but let's see — let us dig some more and try and complete the skeleton.

So we set to with a will. Spades were obtained and, shortly, we were five feet deep and had unearthed another dozen bizarre-looking bones. But we could not find enough to complete the whole skeleton, so, on Monday, we told John McCuish, the Keeper, about this. We walked down together to our pre-historic remains. "Ach," said John, "I buried a horse there a few years ago! "

Under the correct tide conditions in August, the Gerrin Mill Sea Pools were great fun. One started at, or just before, high tide, and gradually worked one's way down the estuary as the water ran out and eventually individual sea pools were formed which contained sea trout up to eight pounds weight. These fish often took your Teal and Silver readily, but the seaweed invariably constituted a big hazard, and hand-lining was sometimes found necessary. As the fish lay on the fine sand in two or three feet of water, it was extremely exciting to watch them follow your fly as you pulled it in towards you; quite often, of course, the fish turned away when only a few feet from you.

One day I was out with G.-H. and John McCuish with our guns; suddenly the keeper put his glass to his eye and solemnly announced that the golden plover were 'in." There were hundreds of them on a nearby beach, and we were told that, in these circumstances, we could approach quite near. So we walked towards them until they were about thirty yards away. We clapped our hands and a veritable swarm of these beautiful birds took to the air.

Now, I was not much of a shot, but G.-H. was a very good one. I had been told, however, that one should never fire into the 'brown,' but it was practically impossible not to do so. There were four shots: not a single bird came down! Even G.H. was shamefaced, and John McCuish said never a word.

June and I went to North Uist in 1934 for our honeymoon when we stayed at the Lochmaddy Hotel. In 1936
we went to Baleloch House, Tighary, on the west side
of the island, and on eight occasions up to 1950, we spent
a very happy fortnight there in August, where we were so
well looked after by Miss Macdonald. Our companions
were generally Andrew and my old friend, John Rintoul.
John, I used to know in Glasgow in the early thirties,
and he eventually spent many years in the Sudan with
Andrew, where he became Auditor-General. He is a very
keen fisherman, a brilliant ornithologist, and a charming
companion.

Our 'beat' was termed 'Bayhead Fishings' after the
hamlet of that name some miles south of Tighary, and
consisted of three main lochs: Hosta, just in front of the
house, North and South Eaval with stepping-stones dividing
them, and Grogary.

There were boats on all the three big lochs, and I
learnt how to manage the oars during these years when
fishing alone. After my first year's very amateur efforts,
I wrote the following article for the *Flyfishers' Journal,*
which may amuse some who have also learnt the hard
way.

LOCH FISHING IS SO SIMPLE

Fishing alone for trout from a boat is easy, so they
say. Row to the "top of the drift," just let the wind take
you down the loch and cast your flies below you: no
trees to hook, no wind to beat, no current to worry about
— in fact, just plumb-easy. This, of course, is the loch-
fisherman's propaganda for his sport, but there are many
poor beginners who approach the water's edge with hope
in their hearts, but leave it an hour later in a lather of
raging frustration.

The wind is rather strong, but it is really very simple,
although getting the boat out against the wind is quite

a strain. Ah! Out in the middle at last! You ship your oars, lift your rod, and cast . . . cast what? Cast nothing, of course, as the knot joining gut to line has retreated below the top ferrule. You reach towards the top of the rod and eventually free the line and — bang! bang! — the boat is gently bumping against the stones on the shore.

You pull out again, and lift your rod . . . not very far, as the line and cast are wound round and round the oar. You unwind them, round and round . . . bang! bang! Jove: on the shore already? What a silly wind: you turn the boat round to see if that will enable you to drift parallel with the shore.

You are at last fishing: suddenly a trout boils at your top dropper; you strike; you miss it, and you quickly shut your eyes as the cast whips towards you and lashes itself round the rod. What a mess! You marvel — as you will never cease to marvel, however long you live— at the amazing tangle into which your line has become involved in so short a time.

When at last you have decided, in a fit of temper, to discard the maze of knotted gut and have tied on a nice new cast of flies, the boat is once again quietly banging on the shore — the leeward shore at the far end of the loch. As you pull up against the freshening breeze, you can at least have time to compose your nerves. Anyway, your mind's off fishing for the time being and is contemplating blisters which have formed on each hand, and another rapidly forming elsewhere.

Now! Once again you've reached the top drift, and you cast. Cast what? Nothing, of course: oh! that damned knot again. Having freed the line, and having, in the nick of time, rescued an oar which was surreptitiously sliding into the water when you weren't looking, you begin fishing. Now, SURELY . . . . .

Another fish rises to your tail fly: you hook it. It rushes under the boat and is 'off.' A mild oath escapes

you and you cast again — no, you don't, you're hooked
fast to the keel of the boat. You now swear as though
you mean it (which you undoubtedly do) and, pulling up
your sleeve, and leaning dangerously far over the side,
you plunge an arm into the water and, with great difficulty,
free the fly.

Exhausted, you flop back on the seat and cast again
— no, you don't. One of your flies is fixed in the lapel
of your coat. Not wasting any more time, you yank it
out and, at the very first cast, you see a beautiful golden
fish roll over your 'zulu,' and you feel the hook 'home.'
It's a good one — you must get it, you simply MUST!
It bores down into the depths: down . . . down — then
suddenly there is pandemonium in the boat. The reel
has fallen off your rod with a sickening clatter and is
rolling about in the bilge water, and your line is stretched
in complicated festoons between your foot, the top button
of your jacket, a rowlock, an oar, and, finally, the rod.
Whimpering, you leap forward and try frantically to undo
the cat's cradle. When this is ultimately accomplished, you
are amazed and heartened to find the trout still 'on.' It
plays for a minute or two, and then you stretch forth
your net and gently lift the two-pounder from the water.
It lies inert, half in, and half out of, the net, then drops
with a splash — back into the water. It makes a wild
dash for freedom; there is a sudden check as one of the
free flies fastens into the meshes of the net, then your
rod springs back to the vertical, and all is lost . . . .

No oath passes your lips this time: just a long, low
groan, and, bang! bang! you're now, once again, at the
far end of the loch.

Having rowed like a galley slave against a roaring
gale to the moorings, you step wearily out of the boat
on to a stone which capsizes, and behold: you are standing
in the water up to your waist! With a mirthless laugh,
you grab your gear, and creep slowly homewards.

"Any luck?" greets you merrily.

D

Words fail you, but, instead, a low animal-like noise rises from the very depths of your tortured soul.

: :   : :   : :   : :   : :

One of our favourite lochs was a small sheet of water a few hundred yords beyond Hosta. On the map it is called *Loch an tseoras,* which we eventually discovered is an onomatopoeic name for 'George's'! We have all had great triumphs and corresponding disappointments. There was, of course, no boat, so you inched round the weeds with a normal loch cast, almost always including a black, or a blue, zulu on the bob.

Those thick trout used to rise slowly and confidently and then turn away towards the weeds with an inexorable pull. I would say that we caught more fish in George's over the pound than under — up to about $2\frac{1}{2}$.

Grogary was always a great favourite of mine; it has a boat on it, but I have always preferred to fish it from the shore in spite of having the worst wading of any loch I know. The bottom is of sharp stones which are small enough to move when you stand on them, but heavy enough to lock your lacerated legs in immovable pincers. Just as a parting joke, the final fifty yards at the east end is soft mud: having extricated your tortured limbs from the underwater mass of quarry-stone, you then, with a sigh of relief, take the next step and sink up to your middle in the submerged morass.

On one occasion, I was moving rather incautiously and my right foot was suddenly claimed in a stone vice. My body was moving: my right foot was not. Slowly, and possibly quite gracefully, I subsided into the waves on to my elbows. Water rushed up my sleeves and hot words gushed from my mouth as my rod crashed downwards and the reel smashed itself on the rocks. In a sudden paroxysm of fury and spray, I yanked myself upright and stumbled ashore, where I stood for a full half-minute, water pouring from my sleeves and waders. And what was I watching? Of course, it was just that usual cow chewing its cud at the water's edge, its beady eyes fixed on me scornfully. In fact, it was definitely all the cow's fault.

On another occasion, I would not even blame the bad wading. It was a beautiful day with a gentle zephyr from the west — ideal. I was wading up to the limit and had been intent on casting over some rising trout in front of me with a small, black gnat. The waves were slowly moving across my vision. Suddenly, something on the far shore attracted my attention. Again, it was a cow, stationary. As I watched, I felt myself inclining to the right, and however I resisted the movement, without splash or fuss, I slid slowly and noiselessly into three feet of water. Having watched the dancing waves move across my vision for a considerable time, the sudden act of focussing on a stationary object had the effect of — but need I explain? The result was water, water everywhere, and loss of dignity and temper.

North and South Eaval: although really one loch, the type of trout at each end differs entirely. The southern part has weed growing on its bed, and the trout are, therefore, dark in colour. We did not, in fact, fish this loch very often.

North Eaval, on the other hand, has a sandy bottom and the fish are silver and gold: beautiful trout which play magnificently.

Loch Hosta, in front of the house, is about a quarter of a mile long and some three hundred yards broad: shallow water over golden sand runs out on three sides for fifty yards to the darker, weed-filled centre. By wading up to the knees, one can walk slowly along on the sand and cast towards the middle where the trout rise to one's flies as they move outwards.

I had an amazing experience in Hosta recently. It was sunny, rather cold, and a strong southerly breeze darkened the blue surface of the water. I inched along the weed-edge, casting three wet flies: Peter Ross on the tail, hackle March Brown in the middle, and a Blue Zulu on the 'bob' — all size 12.

Out of the corner of my eye I watched the dozen swans, either up-ended in the weeds, or gliding about in full sail. Suddenly I noticed two birds in the air at the other end of the loch: very large with dead-white bodies and dark wings. They glided down to the surface of the water and then soared up 500 feet to disappear into the clouds. Their wings never moved; they just swayed and swooped and soared on the wind currents and then disappeared from sight. Ospreys.

I was still marvelling at my luck at seeing such a pair of birds outside Speyside, when I had a splashy, violent rise to my Blue Zulu. The trout tore off immediately and did not stop before it had taken 30 yards of backing. I reeled it in slowly. Again, it rushed off. Again, line was recovered. Then the fish went 'dead' — I was in the weeds. Hand-lining was unsuccessful, and eventually the 4 lb, breaking-strain cast suddenly broke just below the line.

A week later I was again fishing in Hosta. This time I saw no ospreys, and had caught two trout of 1 lb. 10 ozs. and 1¼ lbs. I was some hundreds of yards from where I had hooked and lost the big fish a week previously, when there was a good boil, and the trout ran towards the middle of the loch. However, the 'hold' gave after a few seconds and I disconsolately reeled in to see if my flies were in order. They were, but what staggered me was to find attached thereto, the cast I had lost a week previously — Peter Ross on the tail, hackle March Brown in the middle and a Blue Zulu on the 'bob' — all size 12!

Upon reflection, I think the original trout was foul-hooked. When it rose to me the second time a week later, it was (and felt) hooked in the mouth. The hook came away and fouled the original cast dragging from its back, pulling it out.

We never fish in North Uist on Sundays: if one is

there for, say, two full weeks, a rest on one day in seven is a nice change and, in any case, the country and its birds are so fascinating that a picnic with cameras and binoculars is always very rewarding. If fine — and it is often so on the west coast when pouring with rain at Lochmaddy — we take our sandwiches to the sea where the bays of yellow sand sweep round in great expanses for miles on end, with not even a soul in sight. We lie on the pale-green machair and watch the waders strutting up and down the water's edge for their food. The colour of the sea is ever-changing, and at some time, and in varying conditions of tide and light, there is not a shade of blue or green that could not be manifest. Where the thin fingers of land point far out to the Atlantic, the brightness of the near-white sand beneath the machair is quite dazzling.

In the small reed-covered lochs, we quite often see our favourite birds — the dainty red-necked phalaropes. They alight on a lily-pad and then launch themselves into the water, jerking about in all directions, prodding the surface with their little, sharp beaks. They are not at all shy; in fact, I have managed to photograph them *without* a telephoto lens, though the result, it must be admitted, is not up to the Eric Hosking class.

Another bird we love on the island is the fulmar. There is a disused cottage by Loch Grogary and, for the past two years, a pair of them have nested on the top of the chimney stack. At the same time, a pair of starlings have built inside the chimney underneath, and it was very amusing to watch the smaller bird approach the shared nesting-place with food, and then nip down right under the beady eye of the fulmar sitting a few inches away from it. After a little time, the starling would re-appear and fly off to the accompaniment of disdainful chuckles from the larger bird.

I remember once fishing Hosta from the boat, and I suddenly heard a corncrake barking quite close to me.

There he was, sitting on a fence-post twenty yards from me — so near that every time he croaked I could see right down his pink throat. In spite of the corncrake's propensity for keeping one awake all night, we all love the bird and regret his gradual extinction, due to modern farming techniques.

Last year, June was in the car and pulled up suddenly as she saw two of these birds courting on the road. Regrettably, her camera was out of order: it would have made a unique photograph.

In this context, it is amazing how much more can often be seen of wild life from a car, or a boat, than when one is walking. I recollect watching a water rail on a Hampshire chalk stream not five yards from my car. It was busily strutting around in the shallows near a weed bed; on foot, I probably would never have seen it.

One of the best lochs — if not *the* best — on North Uist is Loch an Duin. When we were at Newton Lodge in 1928, it was included in that estate, but now belongs to the Forestry Commission. Day tickets can be obtained and it is a fascinating loch to fish, either from boat or shore. It has an outlet to the sea and quite often one can catch sea trout in it, though seldom have I heard of large ones being landed. I fished it last year with a gillie and I counted no less than 35 swans drifting down-wind like a regatta on the Solent. Most of these were mutes, but there were also a few whoopers.

The brown trout average over a pound but, for some reason, they do not rise well if the tide is high and the water becomes brackish. They play magnificently and ten pounds of fish — and more — can be caught in a day.

About a quarter of a mile east of Loch an Duin, there is Upper Loch an Armuinn. It is only some 150 yards long by 50 yards broad and, of course, there is no boat on it. The wading is, however, fairly good, and the fish are beautiful to behold: fat, muscular trout, ranging in colour from rich gold to scarlet, like a char. They average a full pound up to over two pounds.

I remember a day last year very vividly as a pair of eagles glided round overhead the whole time I was there, and a short-eared owl swept by noiselessly on the hunt. Meanwhile, a thrush sang its heart out on the top of a heather clump! The only trees for miles are the small alders on the little islands where the sheep cannot reach them, and presumably that is where the thrush will build its nest.

The loch adjoining an Duin is forbiddingly known as Dead Man's Loch (I don't know why), and last year I had an unusual experience there. I was fishing with a team of what could best be described as 'standard loch': Butcher on the tail, Teal and Green in the centre, and a Blue Zulu on 'the bob' — size 12. I was slowly pulling in my cast over a spot I know harbours large fish, and as it was jerked towards me, I suddenly noticed a nice trout following the Butcher, its nose but a quarter of an inch from it. Every time the fly stopped, so did the fish. When I pulled in again, the trout followed. Eventually, I, so to speak, ran out of water, and the fly was actually high and dry on a stone. The trout thereupon put its head out of the water and grabbed it like a dog surreptitiously taking a bone off a table! It played very well and weighed 1 lb. 10 ozs.

When I think of these remote lochs, a feeling of peaceful nostalgia comes over me: not a house nor a soul in sight, but just the small waves rolling from windward to lap on the stones beside you on the shore and the heather and the peat hags around you alive with birds. The crowds and the worries and the incessant noise of modern life are all forgotten as you fish there in a lonely world all of your own.

Chapter 4

KINLOCHBERVIE, SUTHERLAND

A mile or two north-west of Lairg in Sutherland there is a signpost which says 'Kinlochbervie: 44¼ miles.' We then know we are near the end of our journey, and, as the car speeds alongside Loch Shin, excitement and anticipation grow. In 1951, of course, it was a pock-marked morass of stones and bog. They have since 'done it up,' and you can get along quite fast, although the fifteen or so miles are rather 'dreich,' and we are glad to see the last of Shin and pass Loch Merkland on our left as the road climbs to the watershed. Loch More appears on our right and then immediately the famous Loch Stack with Ben Arkle beyond. Stack Lodge is passed where the River Laxford flows out of the loch, and a few miles further on, we turn right on to the Durness road, where we stop the car on the Laxford Bridge and get out and have a look at the salmon directly below us in the dark pool.

One evening, some years ago, we were persuaded to go down to Laxford Bridge to see the sea trout running. It was a fantastic sight. The fish were surging up the sea-pool into the river; they were in such a hurry that they were breaking the water's surface like shoals of small porpoises. However, when a gull or other large bird swept close overhead, there was a sudden stampede downstream; the water was shattered into spray as the frightened sea trout bolted towards the sea. When the bird had passed, they recovered their nerves and, once again, proceeded inexorably upstream towards the river and loch, and the burns of their spawning.

The road hereafter twists and turns between the small hills and lochs until we take the left fork at Rhiconich.

We drive carefully along the road cut into the rocks high above the sea, until eventually we climb through the village of Badcall and then down a long hill towards *Loch Innes na ba Bhuie*. When we see this sheet of water, it is our invariable habit to name it out loud, as the Gaelic words flow like water tumbling out of a pool: *Loch Innes na ba Bhuie* (Loch Innes of the yellow cattle).

We skirt it and pass the crowd of fishing-boats huddled together in Loch Bervie, on our left. Immediately we see the Garbet Hotel, Kinlochbervie.

It is a beautiful, cloudless evening, so we drive on for about a mile past Loch Larach on our right, and stop the car at the top of the hill. We get out to drink in the phenomenal view all around us. To the south-east, on the left, the purple-pink ridge of Foinaven undulates away from you; the huge, bald mass of Arkle reclines lazily in the centre, and Ben Stack's sharp peak just upwards on the right. Long tongues of quiet sea-loch stretch towards the mountains between the rugged capes.

Our eyes turn due south down the west coast towards Wester Ross. In the middle distance, the Island of Handa lies dark in shadow: a paradise for ornithologists.

On the horizon can be seen the fantastic shapes of Cul Mhor, Cul Beg, Suilven and — most prominent — Quinag. Ridge upon ridge of purples and browns stretch to this far-off fairyland, flint-clear in the pure air (rain tomorrow?)

To the west, the sea dazzles with the sun's golden reflection — nothing between us and the New World.

Turning to the north, our gaze runs parallel with the coast: glorious white, sandy bays, lapped by the deep blue on the one side and by the pale green grass on the other. You can just discern the top of Cape Wrath lighthouse peeping above an intervening hill.

We used to go down to the fishing fleet as they came in, to view the vast diversity of fish caught: and to watch the tame basking-shark of at least twenty feet in length, swimming slowly around.

It was, in fact, June who saw an advertisement about the Garbet Hotel first in 1951, and we have since visited the locality now possibly a dozen times. I have not been to a large number of hotels, but the Garbet is certainly one of my favourites. Robert Neilson, the proprietor, was factor to the then Duke of Westminster, and, in spite of his major duties, he invariably took a keen interest in his guests. I am sure, however, he would have been the first to own that Mollie, his wife, did the real work! Alas! Robert died some years ago, and Mollie took on full control with zest and efficiency. She died soon afterwards: I shall always remember these two with great warmth and affection.

The food was simple, but quite superb: salmon, fresh, or smoked in their own garden, sea fish (lobsters included) from Loch Clash two hundred yards from the hotel, good Scots beef and lamb, fresh fruit and vegetables. Cream. Warmth. Cleanliness. Charming staff. And — I almost forgot! — sixty-odd lochs and a couple of spate rivers.

The hotel was razed to the ground by fire a few years ago. Mollie had it completely rebuilt in six months and, when one realises that every brick, nut, bolt and piece of glass had to be brought by road from Lairg fifty miles away, you will agree it was quite an effort.

I must admit it took me a few years (at a fortnight a time) to find the lochs really worth fishing, although I am quite certain there must be many of the more remote ones which are seldom — if ever — fished. Certain it is that each and every one of them contains trout of one size or another.

The lochs near the road are, of course, the most popular. There are boats on most of them, and the trout average ½ - 1 pound. But I find I derive the greatest pleasure when walking, three, four or more miles into the hills towards Foinaven and Arkle. I often got lost: so what?

There's a loch every few hundred yards and, who knows what leviathan may be lurking in some puddle?

There is a little 'loch,' aptly called the 'Tennis Court' (it is no bigger), half an hour's walk from the nearest road. Some years ago, a really enterprising chap, *en passant,* threw his flies on to the mirror surface: result? a brown trout of 5 lbs.! There was no spawning burn into the pool, but presumably some altruistic fisherman had caught a 'tiddler' in the large loch nearby, and had tossed it in the 'Tennis Court' for posterity.

Our party each year usually consisted of June, Andrew, John Rintoul and myself. We have invariably had a magnificent holiday, and as we are very ornithologically-minded, a bird list has always been compiled (75 different species has been the average).

We all realise that the sun does not always shine in Sutherland? The rain and wind can be remorseless, but, even so, a day in the hills can be very rewarding, in spite of the greyness and the wet and the hurricane.

I recollect one seeping morning John Rintoul was preparing to face the elements. The sky was raining stair-rods, the wind blowing a gale and the landscape a waste of grey, wet stones and marsh. At last he was ready: 'reel, rod, basket, etc. . . .,' all were there. He then donned a sou'wester, built more for utility than for beauty, opened the front door, braced himself to the raging tempest and disappeared into the maelstrom, muttering to himself again and again "on pleasure bent . . . on pleasure bent."

As a pin is irresistibly drawn to a boy's magnet, so are we fishermen impelled to face the elements in all their savagery: to experience the dire discomfort of water seeping down our necks: fingers, moribund with cold, wrestling with a tangle in the cast: lashing rain in our faces and chill water slopping in our waders. The day can be a nightmare in the experience, but memory's rose-coloured spectacles dim the horror and present it only as an episode for laughter.

Mollie Neilson used to have an open invitation to fish Loch Dionard, out of which flows the river of the same name. In my view, the fishing there is superior even to Loch Stack — but that may be because I have done better on Dionard. It was pouring rain one day, and Mollie asked me if I would like to fish it. Automatic answer.

The visit entailed a walk of seven miles in each direction, mostly over bogs and peat hags. My gillie, Robbie, and I set out very considerably bent on pleasure as, given wind on the loch, a basket was assured. It was raining heavily as we trudged up the river valley, and, after two hours, we encountered a large burn in roaring spate. Now, I was wearing thigh waders, Robbie only normal Wellingtons: could I give him a 'pick-a-back'?

No sooner suggested than done: with a bound that would not have disgraced a panther, Robbie landed heavily on my shoulders, whereupon the ungainly human amalgamation swayed for a moment, then sank slowly down into the foaming torrent, Robbie undermost. In that uncomfortable position we remained some seconds. I could not rise without pushing Robbie's face under to do so: he could not rise because thirteen stone held him powerless. We eventually gained unsteady feet and splashed to the further bank. It was all very hilarious, and we laughed quite a lot. But all the time we knew that it was not really so funny, as we were soaked to the skin, and it still rained remorselessly. Our tobacco and matches were pulp, our sandwiches a soggy mass of disintegrating flannel. I poured water from my camera. I removed the glass from my wrist-watch and poured water from that. We removed all our clothes, one by one, wrung them out and replaced them in grave discomfort on bodies shivering with cold. The only consolation was that the 'bottle' was intact, and a good dram each persuaded us that, having come so far, we might as well continue.

When we arrived at the loch, it was a dead calm. The boat was rowed vigorously up and down chasing puffs of wind, and I had possibly one hour's fishing. In that time I caught a salmon, a grilse and five sea trout, but we were at last driven to the conclusion that any further stay would certainly result in pneumonia. So we strung the fish about our persons as best we could and trudged the seven miles home. No 'pick-a-back' was offered on the return journey.

In 1954, we three boys — sorry: elderly gentlemen of around 40 years! — had a wonderful day on Loch Dionard. With two anglers in the boat with the gillie, we took it in turns to fish from the shore. I had remembered that Robert Neilson told me, when fishing from shelving sand, to cast parallel with the bank, and not at right angles. Andrew and John were a hundred yards out in the loch, catching the odd sea trout, and I began faithfully to cast parallel with the shore. Sure enough, I had a gulping lunge to my No. 8 Peter Ross, and the salmon streaked off towards the boat. There it jumped, to the great consternation of the other two, until they realised it was *my* fish they had seen so close to them!

Alas — that jump threw the hook, but I had proved Robert right. Incidentally, I have always been puzzled why salmon take up the deep water in a river, but on a loch, they prefer the shallow water near the shore — and preferably where there are rocks around. The sea trout has precisely contrary tastes in each case.

That day we kept over half a hundredweight of fish, and, to my own rod, I had a grilse of 5¾ lbs. and nine sea trout = 27½ lbs. Then, of course, came the rub: seven miles back again with the fish draped around us like suspended dumb-bells. The final crunch came over the final half-mile: a climb of a couple of hundred feet to the road. June was meeting us in the car: with our tongues hanging out, we staggered up to find she had drunk the tea and the whisky! There was a good reason for this apparent misdemeanour, but I have forgotten what it was.

However, when we eventually returned to Garbet at

around 9 p.m., Mollie had stayed up herself and prepared our meal of smoked salmon, roast chicken (with Pouilly Fuissé to swill it down), fresh fruit salad and lots of yellow, germ-infested cream — none of your pasteurised gelatine for us! My mouth waters at the thought.

I have never done really well on Loch Stack. I know that wonderful baskets can be obtained, but I am always plagued with dead calms, and by the time I return to shore, my lips are sore whistling for a wind. A few years back, Andrew and I had a calamitous day. I hooked a salmon which immediately sulked directly underneath the boat: my backing was showing, and I therefore calculated that the fish was about a hundred feet below me. Without any apparent reason, the fly came unstuck.

Andrew hooked a monster sea trout: a slow-motion rise to his 'dap,' a slow-motion wallow, and a slow-motion surge towards the western horizon, then . . . . off! No barb to his fly.

I had an unforgettable experience on Stack some years ago. I was fishing the bottom beat about twenty yards from the road. Suddenly I noticed what looked like a large red-brown stoat moving among the stones at the water's edge. It undulated along rather like a snake: flowing over and round the stones, looking for tit-bits. I asked my gillie what it was? He was flabbergasted: it was a pine marten. He added that, in all his life in the district, it was the only time he had seen the animal in broad daylight, although he had, quite often, seen them in the hours of darkness.

In 1960, June, Andrew and I had a week in September at K.B. There is a loch called 'Generals.' A dam was built across a burn and a catchment formed of some three hundred yards length by one hundred yards width. It is full of weeds, and, candidly, I have considered it to be rather hopeless, except just upstream of the dam itself.

Andrew and I took the boat out one afternoon, drifting over the weeds, trying, fairly successfully, to follow the original burn course. I hooked a salmon, but it went straight for the weeds, and bang! My six-pound B.S. gut had snapped. I had one foot of cast left: "Andrew: give be a fly for the last twenty yards." He produced a size 10 Watson's Fancy: I couldn't be bothered to put up another cast for so short a distance. However, third cast later, I hooked another salmon, which, quite naturally, found the nearest weed-bed. I pulled as much as I dared: the fish eventually surfaced, but there were twenty yards of garbage between it and the boat. Greatly daring, I applied increasing pressure, and the 6¾ lb. salmon was unceremoniously skated across the top of the weeds to a waiting net. On further inspection, it turned out that I had a knot in the foot cast!

Another water I love to fish: it is called the 'Dour Loch,' and it is indeed well-named. It lies in the rocky outcrops: deep, dark and remote. You climb 400 sweltering feet to it, panting your very heart out as your legs plunge through sphagnum moss, or scale overhanging peat hags. You then fish this dour loch the whole torrential day, and sometimes you may perceive a suspicion of a rise about mid-day. You may even be lucky enough to hook and land a fish: if so, it is liable to be a good one.

It is this eternal pipe-dream of a large trout in a glass case over your mantelpiece which irresistibly draws me, year after year, to the Dour Loch. After each fruitless visit, I decide 'never again,' only to find myself a few days later, toiling up the hill-side, cursing myself and the loch, to the accompaniment of vigorous slaps as I flay the clegs which alight to suck my blood.

On one occasion, it was actually not raining. As I breasted the hill, I saw the dark water beneath me, the fantastic outcrops of reddish rocks mirrored on its surface. Two red-throated divers suddenly shattered the deep calm and flew off with a raucous quacking.

"My dry-fly today," I remarked to John, my gillie.

He handed me my rod mounted with 4 lb. B.S. gut and a small black gnat, and I turned to survey the half-mile-long loch with but little enthusiasm. Immediately there was a large commotion on the surface thirty yards away, as though a dog had jumped into the water — a rise already! Very surprised, I drew off a long line and shot it towards the widening ripples. The fly lay still and black, and looked like a smut. I watched it. John watched it. The hills watched it. We all waited.

Then it happened. A large slithering object wormed slowly over the fly, and was gone. I tightened and felt the consummate thrill of a heavy fish as it slowly gathered momentum. The reel's note rose as the trout plunged towards the middle of the loch, and I suddenly realised that my backing was running out. The fish still ran, and I began to get anxious. Just as I glanced down to my drum, the trout stopped and turned. I reeled in furiously to try and retain contact, and soon I was back on my line. We then saw the fish for the first time — definitely the subject for quite a large glass case.

"The net will hardly be big enough, John. We will just have to try it and see." The trout then played like a salmon, sounding deep down and resorting to that nerve-racking 'jagging' as it flung its head to and fro. Eventually, I forced it to the surface and steered the now exhausted body towards the waiting net.

John had netted thousands of trout, but this one was too big for him and my net. It just would not go in. I hung on and watched the huge speckled body balancing on the front end of the net. As John lifted, the fish flopped back into the water.

"I'll bring it round again, John," I said, gallantly. Empty promise! The fish swam slowly a few yards and then — it was off! OFF! No break; the fly was still there. John said something, but I just stood for a few moments watching the reflection of the clouds on the mirror surface. I then subsided on to the heather. Instead of crying, I

1 Glen Sannox and Cir Mhor, Isle of Arran

2. The author, in a snow storm, on the River Spey

3. The author's son, Piers Blaikie, on Brown Burn, Isle of Arran

4. The keen fisherman! My late friend, Teddy Deane, becalmed on
Loch Doilet, Argyllshire

5. Bridge of Alford,
   River Don. Perfect
   trout water

6. Fetternear, Kemnay,
   River Don

filled and lit my pipe — much more grown-up. Without uttering, I rose and cast again into the loch, and immediately there was a boil at my fly. Without emotion of any kind, I hooked, played and landed a trout of 1lb. 10 ozs., with the same detachment of mind and with the same automatic efficiency as one ties one's shoelaces each morning. 1 lb. 10 ozs. I laughed then; but it was a noise without humour, just the poor breathless croak of a fisherman who had met his great opportunity — and lost.

How often it is that one trails away over the mountains with the idea that, because a loch is remote, it must necessarily be better than those nearer at hand? In 1964 I walked towards and round Loch Sandwool after brown trout: all I caught was one decent fish of 1½ lbs. June met me at the road end beside Loch Blarmor. There are a few houses round this small sheet of water, and I think this is probably one of the reasons that the Garbet Hotel guests do not fish it very often. I have always liked it: a good size of trout in excellent condition.

I said I wanted a cast: she said she would return to the hotel, have a bath, and come back for me in half-an-hour. This she did: I had three trout 1.7, 1.8 and 1.9. They played like tigers and were golden beauties. Flies? my diary says Butcher (10), Greenwell (12) and Zulu (12).

One beautiful evening, I was fishing on Blarmor with a small black gnat: there was a fair ripple, and I suddenly saw a lovely head-and-tail rise about 40 yards out in the middle of the loch: how to cover it (I didn't have a tournament rod and line!). So I cast my maximum length towards the rise, but, of course, was still some yards short. I then drew off a yard of line from my reel and 'waggled' the point of my rod. The slack was thus transferred to the water, and, in a few seconds, the breeze had taken line and fly a further yard towards the trout. By repeating the operation a number of times, it was eventually very

E

gratifying to see the little black speck on the water engulfed in a swirl, and the fish was landed after a good fight: 1½ lbs. Nothing very original about this tactic, but oh, how satisfying!

In 1951, one glorious evening, our whole party had a wonderful hour's entertainment. Besides my usual friends, we had, as our guest, June's sister, Lyndsay. She is quite keen on the fishing game, but, let us be charitable, not very experienced. After an excellent dine and wine, we decided to saunter forth and have a cast on Larach — a lovely little loch quite close to the hotel, on which they have a boat. So, away we went, and all five of us crowded into the 12 ft. craft, and, with two rods aboard, started fishing.

We were in rollicking mood: the evening was made for it. Brilliant golden light on deep blue water: the brown hills tumbling down to the dark peat hags surrounding the loch.

It was practically a dead calm, but I hooked a very nice trout on the wet-fly and handed the rod to Lyndsay. Then the fun started. We all simultaneously shouted instructions: "Rod up! Reel in you fool! Let it go! Look out . . . !" As the crescendo of instructions rose, so we gradually subsided into laughter, and the boat was in imminent danger of shipping water, as it heaved up and down like a cork in a rough sea: five large people overhanging the gunwales, all shouting and laughing.

It eventually dawned on me that the chance of winning the battle with four captains and a crew of one was somewhat remote, so, much to Lyndsay's consternation, I snatched the rod from her, and gave it to June, who really doesn't require much instruction.

At last, the fish evidently decided to give up the unequal struggle, and it was netted, and weighed: one ounce short of two pounds. We then sat haunched up and sighing and giggling and lighting pipes and cigarettes on that mirror-calm loch.

The most famous loch in the district is Sandwood: a sheet of water a mile long by a quarter wide. It empties into the Atlantic over a shallow shelf of rock. You can take a car only so far: it involves possibly three-quarters of an hour's walk in both directions along a track, or over the moors. My father's friend, Harry Plunket Greene, mentioned in my chapter on the Don, used to have a cottage on its shores. Alas! No one lives there now, but there is something eerie and fey about Sandwood. There is a popular local story which recounts tales about mermaids, and there is always a queer smell of foxes, which abound in the district.

One painstaking Sunday, we went over to Sandwood to try and scoop the outlet with our bare hands to give the loch a sea-pool. Our finger nails were worn down to the quick, and we had excavated quite a reasonable area. But, in no time at all, nature had filled in our noble work, and it became clear that, short of a bulldozer, no man's efforts could achieve our object.

The fishing for salmon and sea trout can be good — particularly for the latter. Andrew and I had a day there a few years back, and, although not very successful in landing the fish we had hooked, we certainly had plenty of sport. And exercise, too: as there was a near gale blowing, we had to take an oar each to return to the moorings, and we were dead beat by the time we got there (see photograph).

A day on that beautiful loch is a perfect experience for all who love fishing, and the gloriously wild country to which it takes you.

My real personal favourite, though, is named un-romantically 'No. 3.' A cascade of lochs tumbles down the wild and remote valley, the highest being Usaine Uaine ('The Small Green Loch'): but who can remember — or want to remember — such a name? (I do!). So that became No. 5, and the chain of lochs below were numbered from, so to speak, bottom to top.

Andrew and I once went up to No. 5 many years ago. It was like a fairyland: deep, clear, blue crystal water, set in a bowl of brown-red precipices on three sides of us; a ribbon of waterfall slowly tumbling down from the heights over a bed of bright green, weed-covered rocks into the loch below. It was a dead calm and we caught nothing worth keeping, although Robert Neilson told us that some of the largest char to be found in the British Isles inhabited its dark, cold depths. There was a remote eeriness about the place — we could practically feel the quietness there.

No. 3 is possibly the biggest loch of the chain, containing myriads of trout 4, 5, or even 6, to the pound. But, where the burn enters from No. 4, the fish are quite different. The water flows in over golden sand, and the good fishing is only 100 yards each side of the entrance. It takes you an hour to get up there from Rhiconich, and three-quarters of an hour down again — for an obvious reason. The wind is often 'variable.' The big trout can be seen sucking down the naturals — generally just out of casting distance! But you can wade slowly (yes, wade slowly and quietly) about, and have wonderful sport. I usually retain fish of about 10 ozs. and above. My Blue Zulu on the 'bob' seems to be an irresistible attraction to the 'teen-agers,' and when, after a few minutes, you have returned the lively youth to his element, you will have to wade ashore and spend the next ten minutes unravelling the cast.

We caught about half on dry and half on wet in No. 3. A dry Baigent (that wonderful ubiquitous dry fly) or Greenwell does very well. But the best of all is that little, double-tied, black-hackle fly on No. 16 hook: a wonderful floater, and trout gobble it up. I find it deadly on Scottish loch in the calm, or gentle wave.

The last time I went to No. 3, it was a glorious, sunny day. The most memorable thing about it (the basket wasn't terrific; 11 fish = 9 lbs.; best 2 lbs.) was a pair of

eagles wheeling round above me all day. And striding
down in the evening towards the sunset and feeling that
inexplicable happiness and peace.

On two recent occasions, we have accepted the warm
hospitality of the late General Osborne who had a delightful Lodge at Oldshoremore (two or three miles beyond
the hotel). The cream of his fishing was undoubtedly a
salmon loch which lies north and south between the
mountains and the sea. My gillie and companion was
Noah, who, most regrettably, died the following year.
Apparently he was dubbed 'Noah' on the first day he
went to school as a little boy: it lashed with rain remorselessly, and he was called that ever since! He had had
long experience, and he never lost his youthful keenness
and pawky sense of humour — one cannot ask for more.

The loch is about a mile long with a waist in it half-
way up. Here it is some twenty yards wide, and the water
flows sluggishly, and is effectively a slow river. This is
the best place in the loch, and the fifty yards or so of
fishing here is fascinating. There is generally a good head
of small salmon of from 5 to 15 lbs. weight. We always
try this part first, having pulled the boat up on the right
bank. We inch along the shore, fishing the thirty yards
very carefully, waiting for that boil to the little Silver
Doctor, or Jock Scott, or Hairy Mary.

On one particular day, I fished the narrows very
carefully, but I had no rise. A gentle breeze stroked the
surface of the water from the south-west, and the wastes
of mountain and moor around us looked over-bright in
their yellows, purples and browns. It was good to be there,
and it would have been even better if the fish were rising.

When I had finished, Noah suggested a nearby pool.
It was not one in the normal sense. It was called the
Minister's Pool: sometime later it assumed a nostalgic
worth, as I found out that the Minister referred to was
no less than our Foreign Secretary in 1914, the peerless
Earl Grey, who had often fished there with great success.

For some reason — possibly for the chance of a sea trout — I mounted a tandem Black Pennell, size 10, on the 'bob,' and a No. 8 Jock Scott on the tail.

We began the drift, and, from then on for about an hour, I had a rise at almost every cast, and for the rest of the time, I was playing fish. The sequence of events was the same each time. My Pennell was dibbling across the surface. A salmon's snout cleaved the waves behind it. It came short. It came again and missed again. By this time, my rod was almost vertical, and my line stopped and my Jock Scott anchored in a salmon.

In this hour, I rose about twelve and hooked seven salmon. One fish, obviously foul-hooked, rushed off fifty yards of line, jumped, and broke me. Another fish came unstuck. The other five were landed and weighed between 6 and 9½ lbs. each.

Each time a salmon was hooked, Noah pulled to windward out of the area, and there the battle was played out and the fish eventually netted into the boat. Then we drifted back to where we had left off. I cast again and watched the Pennell hopping across the waves, knowing that, at any moment, a dark nose would lunge after it.

Not once during that hour did I have a rise to the tail-fly without rising the salmon first of all to the dropper. It would seem, therefore, that the Pennell provided the shop-window only. Once the fish was interested, it attacked the Jock Scott. Now and again the fisherman is lucky enough to have trout rising to him at every cast on a loch. But when the same thing happens with salmon, the excitement is tremendous, taking the middle-aged man back forty years and more when such thrills electrified him as a boy.

Writing all the foregoing about K.B. has covered some months at an hour or so at a time. I have re-whetted my appetite for this country and all it means. It has that wonderful sense of isolation and peace that North Uist engenders, yet in a curiously different way. The Hebrides is the country of the sea and the green machair, and, although K.B. has both, it is mainly the blue inland lochs among the pink granite mountains that draws me there. One's horizon is as much vertical as horizontal: the eye travels from your feet in the loch to the peat hags and up on to the moor, and yet again up to the heather, and, ultimately, to the near 3,000 ft. summit of Foinaven.

The rough expanse of mountain and loch all around you seems, in some curious way, to reflect a vibrant, golden light, so that the rich colours appear lambent and alive; a glowing panorama as far as the eye can see, softening to the distant, misty blueness of the hills shimmering thirty, or more, miles away.

When shall I next feel the sudden thrill as I read on that signpost 'Kinlochbervie: 44¼ miles'?

CHAPTER 5

NORWAY: ITS COUNTRY AND PEOPLE

I'm silly about Norwegians — I know it. This, of course, is due, not only to their national characteristics, but also to their beautiful country and fabulous fishing.

I have been mesmerised all my life by the grandeur of mountains. I must have inherited this from my mother who was similarly afflicted and who climbed the Matterhorn when she was over 50. I used to do some rock-climbing in my youth and still love to scramble up the hills in Scotland. I think I have about the worst memory for figures of anyone I know, and yet I can rattle off the heights of mountains all day: *not* the most useful adjunct.

To glide on the deep, placid fjords and to look almost vertically upward to the towering buttresses above me, is something of which I will never grow tired. The slender waterfalls ribbon from the dizzy clefts, thousands of feet up, to dissipate into fine spray as they slowly float down the precipices to the fjord below. The huge rock masses rear upwards to the snows, and no man's foot has trodden these walls: a wilderness of rugged desolation and utter peace.

The Norwegians are the children of this land. Their eyes have that far-away look of men accustomed to wide vistas and distant horizons. They have the innate honesty and engaging simplicity of a People who are very thin on the ground, and are not for ever milling around in crowded streets and stuffy business premises. Of course, they have their towns: but I always have the impression that even the town-dwellers' mentality is secondary to their ancient and true heritage of People of the Mountains. There is nothing quite so characteristic to me of Norway and Norwegians as the music of Greig: simple, nostalgic, almost eerie and redolent of the wilderness of vast space.

I accompanied my father to Norway on three occasions: in 1929 to the Evanger, and 1932 and 1935 to the Lærdal. When he died in 1936, an era of Andrew's and my life died with him. The war followed soon after, and it was more than twenty years before, once again, we visited our beloved Lærdal, where there are still those who recollect Dr Blaikie with nostalgic warmth, although it is forty years since he cast his delicate line over the sea trout there.

I shall, in the next chapter, tell of my visit to the Evanger river. This was forty-six years ago, but it all seems as if it were yesterday. Such is the value of keeping a fishing diary; one's memory is thus evergreen and one can re-live and re-live yet again those glorious days of youth, freedom and happiness.

CHAPTER 6

NORWAY: EVANGER RIVER

I was only eighteen years old when I made my first visit to Norway — to the Evanger river, beside the Oslo-Bergen railway. It is big, and some of the main pools require boats to cover the water. It flows out of the lake at Voss, and, some ten or twelve miles further down, empties into what can best be described as a fresh-water fjord at Evanger. After a few miles, it again reforms as the River Bolstad, of which so much has recently been written. The fishing on this latter river for many years belonged to the late C. M. Wells, who was a great friend of my father. He had a fantastic record of large salmon. Anything below 30 lbs. was considered 'a small fish.' This wasn't putting on airs: as far as I can recollect, Wells caught over forty salmon over 40 lbs. to his own rod, and specimens to 65 lbs. plus.

I recollect a friend of Wells telling me an amazing story of a fight with a large fish. Apparently, one of the best lies for salmon is the 'osen' of the lake — just above the start of the river. Wells was fishing with a fly from a boat when he hooked a monster. Now, seldom, if ever, was it found necessary to follow a fish down into the river: it was nearly always gaffed in the lake.

However, this time it was different. The huge salmon bore down into the top pool of the Bolstad, and the boat had to follow. Skilful oarsmanship enabled them to survive the rapids below, and still the salmon plunged onward. After over an hour, they had travelled the whole mile of the river and were entering the final pool: the fish went one side of a large rock, and the boat went the other . . . catastrophe.

Wells never used to recount this epic tale in public,

but my friend said that the fish was estimated to be over 100 pounds; quite possible, as salmon of this size have since been netted in Norway.

I fished the Bolstad one day with my father as Wells' guests. We rowed down from Evanger between the towering mountains while my father whistled old Scottish tunes (he whistled beautifully). That eerie echoing round the dark valleys is quite unforgettable.

As a matter of fact, we caught nothing. The river was very high and coloured and there was half a gale blowing. I remember I was walking back to lunch with my host, and he stopped to watch my father two hundred feet below, where he was casting against the strong wind. "By Jove," Wells said, "your father certainly casts a most beautiful line." Thereupon a loud 'crack' floated up to us as the top half of the rod flew twenty yards to windward to splash into the water.

"Oh dear . . . . ," Wells ventured. It was said with great restraint, but some feeling, as it was his own rod he had lent my father!

On the draft copy of these notes, which I sent to Andrew for comment, I noticed the following cryptic remark in his hand-writing: "I see you don't mention the Bordeaux you had for lunch!" All right: I'd better mention it.

C. M. Wells was one of the greatest connoisseurs of claret in the U.K., and he always kept a very fine 'cellar' at Bolstad. Incidentally, during the war, he kept it well hidden from the Germans underneath tons of potatoes, and when he returned in 1946, his cache was intact — and, indeed, considerably matured.

During this particular luncheon we partook of a wide variety of pre-1914 vintages, and my father afterwards said, with an indulgent smile, that it was the only time he saw his eldest son the worse for drink!

While thinking about C. M. Wells vividly recalls to my mind a little dinner party my father gave about the year 1928. I was 'allowed down' for the first time in a new dinner jacket, and even my mother was excluded while she busied herself seeing that all was going smoothly in the kitchen. We had two guests: Wells and Lord Macmillan, who was at that time a Lord of Appeal. The conversation was fascinating while the young Blaikie goggled in silent awe at the three others as they spoke.

The dinner I recollect was quoted on a menu card with the wines down the centre and the food at the side. We had three late Victorian clarets (one was 1887), and we finished up with two ports spanning a hundred years— 1820 and 1920! The first looked like pink gin (and, as far as I remember, tasted like it); we just had a sip for interest's sake, and then we drank a glass or two of the 1920. Port connoisseurs will doubtless recollect that the wine of this year was very fast-maturing and was quite drinkable six years after it was bottled. This fact, however, was rather a sad matter for me as my father had laid down six dozen for my 21st birthday in 1932. Alas, when the great day arrived, there were only six bottles left!

I have rather a nice entry in my diary for 10th August: " . . . rest of family arrived with Mr Mayou. Latter got salmon on prawn in Ho Osen = 37½ lbs. Daddy one in Skorve Osen on fly = 32½ lbs. Nice fish these." What a patronising youth I was!

The single-line Oslo-Bergen railway ran beside the Evanger, and we used a drasin to take us up to, and down from, the top pools. It was one of those four-wheel platforms which could run on a railway track. A vertical handle was oscillated to and fro for propulsion. We had always to be accompanied by a railway official: a big, red-faced, gruff individual who spent most of his time consulting his turnip to see if the Oslo express was in the offing. We could sometimes hear the distant hoot of the train away up the valley. The railwayman would immediately stop 'rowing,' and press the elementary foot-brake which merely applied direct pressure on to one of the wheel rims. We would stop, lift the contraption off the rails, watch the belching train pass (in all the world like a 'wild-woolly-west' film in the Rockies) and then, so to speak, remount.

One day Andrew and I had great fun (brutes that we were). I don't know what had got into us, but we were flying down from the top pool at a terrific speed, the 'joy-stick' oscillating backwards and forwards like a giant metronome gone berserk. Suddenly, our taciturn friend between us consulted his watch; it told him solemnly that the express was due. Sure enough, a low hoot floated down the valley towards us; the official applied the foot-brake. But Andrew and I still pumped furiously and no amount of foot pressure could reduce our breakneck speed. Our friend's face grew suffused and unintelligible Norwegian words gushed from his mouth. By this time, the two irresponsible Blaikie boys were convulsed with laughter as we plied our not inconsiderable strength to the 'joy-stick.' We careered round a corner, only to be confronted with about half a mile of rock cutting, where it was obviously quite impossible to dismount and let the train through.

The railwayman, suddenly silent in dire anguish, took his foot off the brake and put his podgy hands over ours—and we all pumped, literally, for dear life. We cleared the cutting, stopped and removed the machine just as the iron monster swept round the corner behind us, hooting menacingly.

We did not play this trick again.

I was fishing the top pool one day with Carl Ho, probably the best gillie I have ever met. One fished from a boat, and the way in which he manipulated the oars so that your fly swam correctly, was a revelation.

I had hooked a salmon on a Silver Doctor, and eventually we landed on the staging immediately below the railway. Suddenly the Oslo express came round the corner. Brakes were applied, and the audience watched for five minutes as a 23½ pounder was gaffed: a couple of toots on the whistle, and the train pulled away.

We also had a very delightful companion, Edvard Gjetle. I hope he still flourishes. He should, as he was a very young man in 1929. He was extremely keen to learn English, and had obviously received his grounding from an American, as all his phrases ended with the pronouncement " . . . I guess! " One day I was proceeding to an intermediate pool with him in the horse and trap, and he suddenly asked: "Tell me, Mr Francis, vot is de difference between de 'shoot' which you wear (plucking his coat with his fingers), and to 'shoot' with de gun — bang, bang! " Yes, I know, Edvard, the English language is the Devil!

The fishing was partly fly from boats and occasionally from the bank at the smaller pools, and the rest was harling with spinning prawn. I had a 36-pounder by the latter method, but it is, as I see it, pretty poor sport. My fish, in fact, was exactly four feet long, and, according to the condition-factor chart, it would have been 48 lbs. when it entered the river.

I remember one calm morning when the horizontal wisps of cotton-wool cloud hung round the summits ('good for prawn,' they used to tell us). I was waiting at the water's edge to be rowed across to the railway for transport via drasin to the top pool. I had a dry-fly on my trout rod, and had a cast with it into the calm shallows to see how it looked. A smolt thought it looked good, and I was hand-lining it in when I saw a nasty-looking predatory fish following it. It grabbed the unfortunate smolt, and I crouched down and actually landed a 1½ pound trout which was not even hooked. I felt really virtuous in killing it — a beastly cannibal with a head like a pike, a body of an eel and an enormous tail: it should have been 3 lbs. if in condition.

One day my father caught two salmon on the fly: one a little runt of 4 lbs., the other a noble brute of

40½ lbs. The Evanger certainly holds a large number of salmon of all sizes, and you never know what weight of fish you are going to hook next.

We fished the lowest pool (Skorve) from a boat, and it contained char besides salmon, sea trout and brown trout. Andrew particularly had excellent sport, drifting between the two islands after the char.

This far-off introduction to Norway, whetted my appetite for the land of the mountains, the clear glacial waters, the charming people . . . I was destined never to return to Evanger to fish: from then on, it was the Lærdal: the river of the large sea trout hovering on the golden stones, and waiting for our big, fuzzy, dry-fly.

CHAPTER 7

NORWAY

LÆRDAL RIVER: PRE-WAR

The Lærdal flows into the east end of the longest
fjord in Norway: Sogn. You are then 120 miles from
the North Sea and precipices fall clear into water many
times deeper than anywhere between Norway and Great
Britain. The village of Laerdal lies tranquilly at the river's
mouth — old-fashioned, wooden-housed, with just one
long street down its centre.

I must hasten to add that, correctly, the village is
called Lærdalsöyri, which means the delta of the Lærdal
river. Lærdal is a district, not a town; but with typical
British inaccuracy for foreign place-names, we have always
referred to Lærdalsöyri as Lærdal, and I, therefore, have
followed this erroneous nomenclature henceforward in the
next two chapters.

As you make your way upstream, the valley closes in
to sometimes less than half a mile. Your eyes follow up
the spruce, alder and juniper-covered walls on each side
to the rims of the gorge three thousand feet above you.
Waterfalls tumble from the high tops, striking intervening
rocks in explosions of fine spray which slowly float away
like mists at daybreak.

After a few miles, you will come to Seltun where
the valley walls are no more than fifty yards apart at
the narrowest, the river plunging down in a foaming flood,
occasionally widening out to a deep, clear pool in which
you can see every boulder — and often grey shapes of
salmon and sea trout, their tails waving gently in the
slow current.

There is a pool there with the road directly fifteen

7. Loch Hosta, Tighary, Isle of North Uist

8. The author's wife and "Cheeka" at Lochmaddy

9. Loch Garbet Mhor and Ben Arcuill

10. "Number 3" Loch and Foinaven

11. The author together with his father, Knut and their catch, Lærdal, 1932, 40½ and 18lbs.

12. 11lb. sea trout

13. The Horse Pool, Hauge
    Beat, Lærdal

14. Andrew with an 11¾lb
    sea trout, Lærdal

feet above. No wading for you would walk into twenty
feet of icy water. Mr Seltun told me, when we passed it,
that my father was the only person he had ever seen, who,
from that position, could drop his fly 25 yards away under
the rocks on the far side. "Why not have a try yourself?",
he asked. I declined. It would have been shattering, whatever the result. I still hold to the view that I could not
possibly have done it.

Proceeding upstream, the valley becomes narrower
and narrower, until you reach the foss: a plunging cataract
of pale green water up which no migratory fish can pass.
The width between the vertical walls here will only be
some ten yards, and a boiling cauldron sweeps away below
you to a deep, clear blue pool full of salmon and sea trout
which are always trying the impossible — to scale the
foss water above.

I have heard of an interesting poaching technique
here, which, of course, is highly illegal. At one time,
before the value of the fishings in the river had been
realised, they used to lower a small boat into the pool,
and white, vertical streaks of paint were brushed on to
the walls. The fish would then, having been defeated by
the force of waterfall above, have a jump at what they
thought were lesser waterfalls on the rock sides. Having
thus stunned themselves against the rock-face, they were
collected by the enterprising 'fishermen' stationed at the
foot of the pool as they floated by them.

My father took me first to the Lærdal river in 1932.
It was a glorious August, and it was the only time I
have spent a full month's holiday there: one advantage
of university vacations! We were fishing on the Mid-Lysne
beat, some six miles up from Lærdal.

I have found that, with nearly all fishermen I have
met on this river, it takes a season or two to get to know
how to fish reasonably efficiently for sea trout with the
dry-fly. I do not really know why this is. There are those
experts of the English chalk streams who should be

F

immediately successful, but somehow the habits of the sea trout are quite different. Their reactions to danger are not the same. For instance. in a chalk stream, an alarmed brown trout will take cover in a weed bed. In the Lærdal, there are, generally speaking, no weeds at all, so the fish merely sidles into the middle of the river and will not take anything. There is also this fact. On a river the size of the Lærdal, very long casting is a necessity. The fish may be thirty yards plus away from you, and if you are within its angle of vision, it can see you.

On a chalk stream there is very often a predictable rise. On the Lærdal you can seldom tell if a fish will rise or not; neither will it come more than once, except in very rare circumstances.

The fly we generally use these days is one so aptly named "Shaving Brush," not unlike our loch dapping flies, and either black and white or brown, size ten hook. However, particularly in the early visits before the war, we caught them on large Tups, Red Palmers, Mayfly or even a Baigent — the last an exile from the River Don. Doubtless practically any dry-fly would catch fish as long as it floats high on the water and does not get drowned.

We generally use a 6 lb. breaking strain nylon cast, and sometimes in very bright water, even this is on the thick side. The sea trout are very gut-shy and if, for instance, the final three inches just above the fly will not lie flat on the water (an annoying habit), it will not look at you.

One day in 1932, I was walking down with my gillie, Knut Ødegård, and in the bright, sun-soaked conditions, the river was abnormally low. We passed what seemed to me rather a likely-looking run: popply water flowing slowly over sand-coloured stones and about four feet deep. What about it? Knut was doubtful — "never seen it fished before." However, I started at the bottom with a large Tup and suddenly a blue-grey snout appeared, sucking my fly under. The fish played very well, taking out fifty yards of line in two long runs. Eventually the sea trout raced down and across stream, and I had to follow. I did indeed wade the river (a rare possibility) and when I looked round, Knut was nowhere to be seen. Suddenly he popped up from the depth of the pool, brandishing his gaff above his head! There was no beach on the right bank, and he made no mistake with his first shot: a 10½ pounder was borne, struggling, to the shore.

I tried again next day: another one of 9 lbs. So this short stretch of water was named 'Francis' pool and, apparently, the name has stuck. This is something of which I am very proud.

In those days when I was my father's guest, we would have a gillie each, and it was usually the custom to fish a pool up for sea trout with the dry-fly, change rods, and cast for salmon down again. We fished for salmon with all the usual flies of the period: 'Thunder and Lightning,' 'Black,' 'Blue' and 'Silver Doctors,' 'Black Dose,' 'Lady Caroline' (for low water work), 'Jock Scott,' and so on.

When the water was high and dirty, we would try spoon or shrimp, and, during the final week before the closing of the season (4th September then, 31st August now), we would prawn the pools for the first time. By then the salmon had, in any case, become rather stale and red, and it was very difficult to move them with the fly. But the first time they saw the prawn, they were wild for it. We might do well for a couple of days or so, but suddenly the fish seemed to grow tired of it, and, apparently, become actually frightened. Many's the time towards the end of our stay when a prawn cast among the salmon would send them dashing downstream out of the pool altogether.

On the 2nd September, 1932, I had a great day with the prawn, and I had my first article published in *The Field* the following spring. I think it is worth quoting in full.

"Seldom has it been my lot to become blasé when fishing for salmon. It is a condition few fishermen are lucky enough to experience. We spend many hours dreaming of that one glorious basket, and, where salmon are concerned, we thrill at the thought of two, three or more silver shapes lying on a green bank. When at last the dream-day arrives, it is rather a shock to find oneself suffering from sheer boredom, becoming heavy-handed with the fish, and inwardly rather disappointed when the next salmon turns the scales at a mere ten pounds.

It was such a day at Lærdal when my father and I were having six casts in turn, as the fish were taking so well! It was nearly our last fishing day, and we were prawning our best pool (Mid-Lysne) for the first time. It had yielded twenty-seven for the month, and all those on the fly. It was about three o'clock in the afternoon on a clear, bright day. The river was abnormally low, leaving on each bank, heap upon heap of great yellow stones, varying in size from a hen's egg to a boulder of many tons. We had already hooked between us ten fish, landing five up to 25 lbs. I had just taken over the spinning rod, my father having had his 'six.' He said he would go below with Knut and see if he could pick up a sea trout with the dry-fly.

I hooked something big on my first cast. But, you see, by this time, I was blasé, so I almost literally hauled the fish in. It came into the shallows after about ten minutes, and I could see, as I thought, that it was indeed large. Nils was just about to strike with his gaff, when an amazing thing occurred. The hold in the salmon's mouth seemed to give suddenly, and then as suddenly, catch on again. Nils knew even less English than I did Norwegian, but he did not lose any time in telling me what had happened, as he went frantically through the motions of a monkey scratching his back.

A heavy salmon, hooked in the back and in a powerful stream, does not need any encouragement to fight,

as we know. I had hardly recovered from my surprise, when
the fish was out of the pool altogether. I stumbled clumsily
after it over the boulders, my reel barking as the line
whizzed out in jerks. By the time I had reached the corner
where the river takes a sudden turn to the left, I felt
as if I had run a mile with far too many clothes on —
which was a fair approximation of what I had done!
I could see a huge tail waving in the air as the salmon
bore down the shallow rapids eighty yards away.

By this time I had reached my father, who was rudely
interrupted in fishing his favourite bit. I was just passing
him and puttitng on all the strain I could, when 'snap,'
my greenheart rod broke a few inches above the reel!
Like lightning, the broken rod top sped down the line
towards the fish. But Knut was even faster. A young, fair-
haired, excitable Norwegian lad, he jumped from my
father's side, dashed into the torrent up to his waist, and
caught hold of the fast-retreating rod top.

The following five minutes will always remain in my
memory as containing the largest complement of humour
and excitement I have ever experienced, or am ever likely
to experience. The fish, with Nils running along the bank
beside it, gaff in hand, waiting for an opportunity to make
a lunge, was now out of sight round the bend in the
river. Knut was in the foreground, stumbling through the
shallows, holding the rod top high above his head — and
I really think gaining some support thereby! Time and
again he stumbled forward, made a terrific splash, but
always seemed to remain upright. And here was I, gasping,
jumping, slipping, holding exactly twelve inches of rod-
butt reverently in front of me, on to which was fastened
a six-inch reel. To my father, who 'also ran' somewhere
in the rear, the sight must have afforded great entertainment.

When at last Knut and I stumbled on round the
corner, imagine our surprise and horror to see a quarter
of a mile of river stretching away from us — and no

Nils! A shout beside us made us wheel round, and there, behind a bush sat Nils, with a colossal grin all over his face — and a 36 lb. salmon at his feet! In a common language of inarticulate sounds — being incapable of anything else — we indicated great elation and thanksgiving, and to the tune of general sighs and weary laughter, we lit cigarettes and lay exhausted on the bank, gazing up into the deep blue above us."

"1st Sept. Seltun and Saer no good. Weather bright and river dead low. Got last salmon left in Obero Bo on way back on Black Dose = 18 lbs. JBB salmon Mid-Lysne on spoon — 40½ lbs. Terrific fish."

This cryptic entry in my diary lets me recollect every moment of that hour, 43 years ago.

My father and I travelled down the valley in the car just before lunch. As we sped along the road, clouds of dust billowed out behind us, while the sun beat down on a river which was a mere trickle compared to its height under normal conditions.

We stopped the car on Bö Bridge and surveyed the pool below. Usually, one could see twenty, thirty or more salmon in their serried ranks stretching down a hundred yards below. But on this day, we could spot only a single, lonely fish half-way down.

"Why not have a cast for him?", my father suggested. As I had on many occasions fished very hard over the heads of twenty or thirty salmon there without success, my personal feelings were inclined to be negative, but a dutiful son (ostensibly of the 'never-to-be-beaten' type), said "Right!" So my father went up in the car to the rapids above Mid-Lysne for a cast with the spoon in the fast water there.

I positioned my gillie, Nils, on the bridge so that he could direct my endeavours towards that lonely salmon half-way down the pool. I went down and started fishing about twenty yards above where the fish was lying. After a few minutes, Nils shouted, "A liten langer down . . he's coming . . . HE'S COMING! . . . ". And 'bang' — the fish was 'on.' It was played and landed: 18 lbs. We walked back to the house for lunch, both extremely self-satisfied. I was longing to see what my father thought . . .

I was somewhat disappointed to find that he had not yet returned. Immediately I noticed him lighting his pipe in a field a hundred yards towards the river. Of Knut, his gillie, there was no sign.

My father walked slowly towards me, and suddenly Knut appeared behind him with an enormous salmon slung over his shoulder, reminiscent of the Scott's Emulsion advertisement.

"That looks a magnificent fish," I gallantly said. "What happened?"

"I lost three complete tackles on the bottom, but the third time, the bottom moved! "

"How big?"

"40½ lbs."

Knut flopped the four-foot monster on the house steps.

"And how did you do?" I indicated my miserable catch.

"Stout lad! " said my father with genuine enthusiasm. I have, however, always regretted that the Fates decreed that my father had to catch such a fish on the same day that I was so proud to land the last fish left in Obero Bo! (See photograph).

In 1935 I went to the Lærdal for the second time, but it was to be the last with my father. I was by then married, and June made her acquaintance with this delightful country. I was only there for a fortnight, and the fishing was not particularly good.

I recollect one episode which still makes June and me smile. One day, after a heavy lunch, my father was having a snooze, while we were larking about on tip-toes and completely silently. Now, there was a magnificent flat, round brass tray on wooden legs in one corner of the room, laden with decanters, beer bottles and glasses. Suddenly one of us staggered in our silent horse-play into this and there was an almighty crash as the whole lot was swept to the floor — decanters spilling out, glasses and bottles rolling about and general pandemonium everywhere. My father woke up with a start, and he was as near being extremely angry as I ever remember him. We stood very still and tried to look contrite, but I still have the feeling that my father knew he should be angry, but couldn't quite make it convincing!

One glorious evening of that year is described in my diary as follows:

"Fished up with dry-fly from 'Bottom Pool.' Hooked a sea trout almost immediately = 3 lbs., then rose another, which missed me. Rose and hooked a good sea trout in 'Old Vold Bridge' above. Played magnificently = 6¾ lbs. Another also there: 1¼ lbs. Fished 'Hew Pastor' and 'Bottom Pool' for salmon — no good. Fished later down again with big 'Dusty Miller' and hooked a salmon. Gaffed in 20 minutes by Martin. Excellent evening's sport: 5 rises; 4 fish."

As I slowly enter the pool at its foot, the background is the vertical rock-face, a quarter of a mile away. The green of the waving apple-trees is bathed in sunlight against the dark precipices; the clear water flows leisurely in front of me and the pale-yellow stones can be clearly seen beneath — not a trace of weed anywhere.

I wade slowly in — only to a foot's depth; a large Tup is cast high up on the main stream slowly heaving past me. It looks good as it sits erect on the surface. I cast again, slightly nearer my bank. Immediately a nose appears, followed by a grey back, then a large tail, and the fly has disappeared. I then — and only then — tighten to feel the satisfactory weight. The fish slowly gathers momentum as it bores downstream past me. I stagger backwards as the reel barks out. The fish at last pauses near the foot of the pool. Suddenly the strain slackens and I reel furiously, trying to keep contact. The trout speeds past me upstream and, once again, the line streaks out . . . and out . . . and out . . .

The fish suddenly leaps high out of the water nearly a hundred yards away, falling back with a tremendous splash, and, once again, races downstream. The line is slack; I reel in as fast as I can. Is it still 'on'? At last I feel resistance, and I can see it boring slowly round and round, twenty yards out. I walk back on the shore stones, leading it in firmly. The trout suddenly realises that it is in the shallows; it rushes away again, but the run is shorter this time, and eventually it stops a few yards out and starts thrashing with its tail and throwing its head from side to side. This is nerve-racking; will the hook hold?

At last it is quiet, and it is gently, smoothly coaxed to the shore and the head rests on a stone just out of the water. I put my rod down, and in three big strides I am between fish and river; a sudden heave with both hands and the sea trout is flapping and jumping on the dry stones, where it is secured and despatched.

With that wonderful feeling of elation, I look down on the beautiful silver shape. It weighs 6¾ lbs. I have caught sea trout nearly twice the size, but it is my experience that, often, it is the six-pounders that give the most exhilarating sport.

I remove the Tup from the roof of the mouth, wash it, re-anoint it, and, once again, creep slowly into the water and start casting above me. The sun has dipped behind the dark precipices on the south side of the valley, its golden shafts flood-lighting the green potato fields and the red and white houses on the other side. The cliffs opposite are etched in minutest detail of stone, juniper bush and delicate waterfall.

I was naturally very anxious to see June land a salmon for me; something which she had never done. Of course, in such cases, one can never arrange the timing right.

When I hooked a salmon, she would be away up the mountains and when she was with me on the river bank, no fish would ever dream of rising to my fly.

However, on the very last day, the river was in turgid spate, and she was with me at Horse Pool while I tried 'shrimp,' the technique being precisely similar to fishing with worm. The bait was swung upstream on a salmon fly rod, quite close to the side, and the shrimp trundled down the swim. Sure enough, I hooked something: "Here you are! " I shouted, handing the rod over to her. The fish played very energetically and June had an exciting time, playing it in a very correct manner. Imagine our chagrin, therefore, to discover on landing the fish that it was a sea trout of 7lbs. 6 ozs.! So she did not land her salmon after all, though, since then, she has, of course, killed quite a number.

An so June, Andrew and I said goodbye to Lærdal for over 20 years, and re-explored our old pastures in North Uist and Sutherland. We missed this delectable river and its charming inhabitants but, as you have already realised in previous chapters, Scotland has, for us, a charm and warmth which adds up to something as rich as the attraction of Norway. This view, I think, is partly a reflection on the people who make up the party. Whether you fish, ski, mountaineer or merely tour around in any part of this world, it is companionship in its widest sense that will contribute the greatest sum of happiness to all concerned, whatever the country and whatever the sport.

CHAPTER 8

NORWAY

LÆRDAL RIVER: POST-WAR

I was having dinner one Thursday evening in the Flyfishers' Club late in 1955, and I was engaged in playing a hand of our brand of light-hearted bridge. Suddenly, a tall, lean bean-pole of a man came in and began talking with those around him. He was to me obviously a Norwegian, and his English was so fluent, it was sometimes difficult to follow him. I quickly got rid of my rubber of bridge and approached him, introducing myself.

"Blaikie," he said, "any relation to Dr Blaikie who used to fish the Lærdal?" This was Aage Rygh, a lawyer by profession, and one of the most eminent fly-fishermen in Norway. It was wonderful to hear about the place again after so many years, and he very kindly invited me to be his guest the following August.

I was lucky enough to spend two holidays with him there, and he was a most stimulating companion. He generally brought with him his charming wife Ellen, and his two children, Pernille and Christen.

Unfortunately, he died in 1963 and I count myself lucky, along with many others, that I knew him and had the opportunity of watching his amazing technique with the dry-fly. When I come to describing the pools which make up the Hauge Beat, I will recount the story of his capture of the record sea trout in Horse Pool. No wonder he did not bother during the last few years of his life to fish for anything but the very biggest. I can picture him now, sitting on the platform in Horse, legs a-dangle, his rod lying flat beside him, awaiting what was in his view, the magical hour of 3 p.m. Then, like a drunken gaucho, he would silently propel his line thirty yards away to those grey shapes in the main current; he was adept at mending his line in the air so that the fly always floated first over the fish.

He never greased his line! He discovered that, although the sea trout would not take a skating fly, it would snatch at one which had suddenly sunk beneath the surface. I don't think he bothered about the fish directly above him. I have tried his method in these circumstances, and it is quite hopeless, as the slack makes it impossible to strike. When the cast is wide out across the current — that is different. The line is at its full stretch; when the fly is about to drag, the wrist is turned over and it plops beneath the surface. So many of the sea trout follow the fly downstream but, of course, leave it when it begins to skate. But if it suddenly becomes 'wet,' they are after it immediately, and the slight belly in the line makes the hooking practically automatic.

Since I went to Lærdal last with Aage in 1962, I have been every year, and the party has generally been the same. The three rods are Knut Apold, my brother Andrew and myself: June generally comes also, but, last year, she had 'back' trouble and V (Virginia), Knut's wife (and June's cousin) came instead. We are hoping this year that both the girls will come.

Knut Apold I have known for some twenty-five years. He came over at the beginning of the war with the French army and was, curiously enough, at one time in my doctor brother's Company in the Parachute Regiment. He married during the war and now lives in Ayrshire, working as managing director of a paper mill. He still carries Norwegian Papers, but he is Scots as an Aberdonian, and, in fact, recently received the Order of St. Olav for his outstanding record of promoting goodwill between our two countries.

He now has a shock of white hair (although still the right side of sixty-five), and he regales us with stories of

the Trolls playing their knavish tricks in the far-off forests
and snowy mountains of Norway.

He comes from Odda on the Hardanger Fjord: how
proud I am to thave introduced a Norwegian to the Lærdal!
I think the main difference between Apold and the Blaikies,
as far as fishing is concerned, is that the former is extremely
keen on this sport. The latter are just mad on it!

I do not need to apologise for re-quoting Plunket-
Greene's remark about my father: "There was nothing he
would not do, fair or foul, to manoeuvre his partner into
the best places." It equally describes Knut Apold's unselfishness, both off and on the water.

As for Andrew: well, he's my brother. According to
my diary, I have fished with him for about 600 days,
stretching over nearly fifty years since we used to yank
the two-ounce brown trout out of the burns in Roxburghshire with worm. He, in my view, is the finest fisherman
I have met (other than, of course, our father). There are
those, I suspect, who know more about entomology. The
'bottom feeders' would beat him hollow when it comes
to dace, chub, tench and the rest; but as a fly-fishing
machine, he has no equal. When an angler gets into his
class, it's not only just the pure mechanics of casting,
nor the hundred-and-one technical details affecting the
catching of salmon and trout; there is some innate sixth
sense which harnesses the fisherman's knowledge and lifts
him clear of the others.

Then there is my wife, June. She, poor darling, had
to spend her honeymoon on a fishing holiday in North
Uist many years ago, so she was, so to speak, thrown in
the 'deep end' straight away. She often says she could
have become very keen on fishing, but she has always
been otherwise engaged in bird-watching, painting, or
merely walking and climbing. I think it is probably the
ideal arrangement in that she is available, and pains-
takingly willing, to act as chauffeur for the fishermen; and,
last thing at night, we see her headlights shining down

the road as we reel up our lines in the gloaming, lift
the fish (if any!), and slowly, contentedly walk across the
field towards her welcoming voice 'any luck?'

V, who came out last year, is also a country-lover,
and it will be great fun if we have them both this year.
On one or two occasions, the Apolds' elder daughter,
Karen, has joined the party — and has caught salmon
in the Lærdal!

It's a most happy and relaxing life we live at Hauge
Farm. There are two houses on adjoining sides of the
steading belonging to the Kaardals, and we occupy the
one on the north side.

John Kaardal is a school-master at Lærdal, two or
three miles downstream at the mouth of the river. His
wife, Anne Sofie, looks after their farm when John is
away, and also tends her three attractive daughters.

Our house has a living-room, kitchen, two double and
two single bedrooms, and (nowadays), a bathroom and
inside W.C. (Andrew made comment when he read this:
"No mention of the communal, multi-holer long-drop of
yester-year? Perhaps not!" Knut, on seeing Andrew's
observation, adds: "Why not?" So there it is, Knut, I've
mentioned it!)

We used to be able to get some 'help' but latterly
this has been found impossible. So Anne Sofie, on top of
all her family duties, cooks our main meal for 1 o'clock.

I am the breakfast king: bacon, eggs in some fashion
and in considerable profusion, and cubes of white bread
crisply fried in hot fat (an idea I learnt from the Americans
in the war).

Then down to Lærdal in Knut's Morris Traveller to
get the 'messages.' One excellent fact about the river in
late August is that the sun does not rise above the
mountains on to the water until around 10.30, and the
fishing — for the sea trout, anyway — is no good until
this time.

We all go along and talk to the butcher's widow (at

least, Knut does, we merely push him forward!). We buy the odd trinket for taking back to the U.K. We cash what travellers' cheques we have. We visit Lindstrom's Hotel for picture post-cards.

Sometimes June has gone down alone to do the shopping. Without practically a word of Norwegian, ingenuity almost invariably wins. She 'moos' for beef, and 'baas' for mutton. However, she certainly met her Waterloo one day. She visited the chemist, and, after some altercation, there was quite a crowd around her *so* keen to help — but, no, she couldn't make them understand what she wanted, and she came out empty-handed. She was, of course, handicapped as she could not use her normal routine: she wanted to buy toilet paper!

Malvin is our most excellent gillie-cum-water-bailiff. He takes our salmon down to Lærdal for smoking at lunchtime, or trout for the deep-freeze. We engage him in turns — generally the one who is fishing a salmon pool receives his services. He is desperately keen and an unerring gaffer.

Generally, however, one can beach all fish, both salmon and sea trout. There are some places, however, where a man with a gaff will make that important difference between a fish and no fish.

We are on the water at about 10.30, and return two hours later. It's a wonderful time of day; the sun is usually shining, the fish are weighed and stories are told over a glass of gin or whisky — oh yes — and the girls come back from school!

At one we have our main meal: an assortment of smorgasbrod on the table, then Anne Sofie comes in with her beautifully cooked meat, potatoes, cauliflower, etc. When you have had your fill and are patting your tummy and saying "Ah" — she comes in again with a duplicate of the dish already consumed! Which we devour with relish, until one of us might say "Ah well: to Wallendahl now." So we all move off to our separate beats with rods in our hands and hope in our hearts.

And while on the subject of food, I think many people would welcome the recipe for *Grav laks (laks =* salmon and *grav,* believe it or not! = grave. By 'grave' we, of course, refer to the cemetery). This way of treating salmon and the larger sea trout is really an alternative to smoked salmon, and Aage Rygh taught me this method in 1958. More recently, Andrew has taken on the mantle of this work, and I think he likes doing it better than anything else — other than, of course, the catching of the fish so necessary for the recipe.

Quoting Andrew:

Fish: Salmon or sea trout (4 lbs. minimum).

Method: Head and tail, and clean with paper *(never* with water). Remove backbone, ribs, pectoral and anal fins. Open out flat like a book and cover flesh with a liberal quantity of salt, a pinch of saltpetre, evenly spread, and a sprinkling of brown sugar. Then lay on flowers and leaves of dill, making sure flesh is well-covered. Fold over and place in a flat-bottomed receptacle and put a clean wooden board on top of the fish, with a few stones or bricks to weigh it down. Cover with muslin or something similar to exclude flies, and place in a cool locality — a cellar is ideal.

After 24/36 hours, turn the fish over, and, after a similar period (i.e. about 72 hours in all), it should be ready to eat. After draining off the liquor, it will keep for weeks in the cool, and for months in the bottom of your fridge (but avoid freezing).

Slice thinly on flatbrod (or, second best, brown bread), with some butter, and add lemon-juice and pepper to taste. It goes exceedingly well with aquavit, or even gin! I feel sure that the U.K. salmonidae would lend themselves just as well as the Norwegian variety; it is a scrumptious delicacy.

However, so much for our background. Let us return

to the river. Having fished all afternoon, we saunter back around six-thirty and eat a course prepared by June or V, or possibly Karen: we will discuss the day's angling proceedings; the birds and the flowers seen by the women —then out again for a few casts in the failing light. The sun is off the river, but its golden splendour is thrown on the north-side precipices. The bats begin to flit around your head, and you mount a single No. 8 or 10 wet-fly and await that savage wrench and the sudden, angry bark from your reel.

It gets dark around 8.30 - 9.30 p.m. in late August, and the rapidity of the pursuing night catching up on you every evening is slightly depressing. We all congregate at the farm when the car returns from the far pools and the fishermen have walked in from Green Bank. The three chaps play furious Canfield Patience to see what is going to be the luck on the morrow (When Knut saw Andrew and me doing this years ago, he was disdainful: he's now contracted the chronic disease himself, although I *have* caught him cheating).

Our father taught us how to score in this game. One starts each hand with minus ten, and receives one for each card 'got out.' So we generally 'have a ten'; in other words, we deal ten hands: if the total comes to more than a hundred altogether, the fishing next day is going to be good, and vice versa.

The worst tragedy that can happen is to get a hand completely 'out' (i.e. scoring 42 points net), and yet be so poor in the other nine that the total is still less than 100! We call this being 'Rubiconed.'

Such a tragedy is rare, but we remember with great amusement, two years ago on the eve of the final day, when this calamity befell me. Andrew and Knut solemnly told me that, on the morrow, I would probably:

      (a)   Fall in,
      (b)   Lose a big fish, and
      (c)   Break my rod.

G

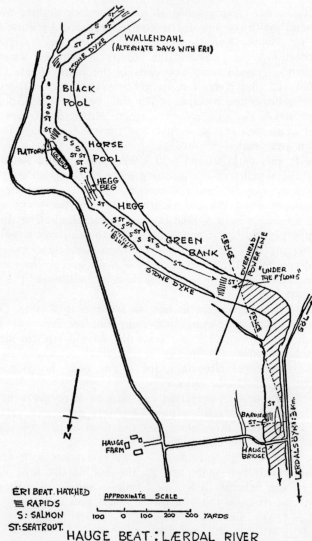

ÉRI BEAT. HATCHED
≣ RAPIDS
S: SALMON
ST: SEATROUT.

APPROXIMATE SCALE

100   0   100   200   300 YARDS

HAUGE BEAT: LÆRDAL RIVER
SOGN

. . . which, in fact, is exactly what happened! And
to add insult to injury, I let Malvin have a cast (being
the final afternoon) on Green Bank, while I went upstream
to suffer the dire adventures quoted above. On the way
back, soaked to the skin, my rod in pieces, and a large
sea trout with a painful jaw recuperating in the middle
of the river, I passed a grinning Malvin who had just
landed a fourteen pounder on the dry-fly.

By 11 p.m. we are ready for bed and, in a quarter
of an hour, we are floating into a deep sleep: tired, happy,
awaiting the dawn of another day — what will it bring?
Will there be a movement of sea trout up the river? Will
that 40-pounder in Hegg take a Blue Charm? Will that
big sea trout in . . . ?

We will now walk down the Hauge beat and have a
look at the pools. The fishing, as is general in Norway,
belongs to the riparian farmers. We have both banks,
although, in most of the pools, it is impossible to cover
the centre of the river whence our large friends retreat
when they have grown tired of us and our flies. It should
be realised that, towards the end of August, the water
is often very low, the glaciers having largely melted and
are awaiting the first snows of autumn. Very hot days
(and we *do* have them) still bring down some fresh water,
and it is this kind of weather which we like — so different
from conditions over here.

Andrew has made a rough sketch of the beat, and
the area between the banks as shown, is generally more
than half taken up with dry stones, and, particularly in
Wallendahl and Hegg, you often have to walk fifty yards
from the grass to the water.

We have the top pool, Wallendahl, on every other
day, sharing it with our neighbours on the Eri beat. It
is a story-book pool with its narrow head widening out
into a lovely sea trout of about three hundred yards. The
main current is close to the right bank, and, in high water,
salmon lie fifty yards down here. Unfortunately, heavy

winter floods have recently tended to alter the pool to its detriment, and it all depends on the head of the fish in the river whether you are going to get a really good day, or a near blank.

Its right bank is not pleasant to fish. The main stream is constantly eroding it, with the unhappy result that the fisherman is always tending to roll down the stones into the water. A couple of years ago, Andrew hooked a very lively sea trout here which tore downstream and underneath a tree which had fallen into the water. So, of course, he followed it — under the tree and all! He eventually scooped it out round the corner above the Black Pool.

There is an appallingly difficult patch of water to fish at the top of the right bank. As there are trees very close to the river here, the only method of approach is from the left bank across the rushing current, which can be accomplished only when the river is very low. Even then, we almost always 'go over the top' of our waders, and, to make matters worse, the fast water near you drags the fly almost immediately after landing on the comparatively slow stream beyond. So we endeavour to cast with as much slack as possible to give those few extra seconds of fishing. Furthermore, if you happen to be here on a fine afternoon, the glare of the sun on the water is such that you cannot see your fly. The area to be covered cannot be more than that of a tennis court, and yet one day I had six or seven sea trout up to 3 lbs. from it.

The final day's fishing in 1962 (31st August) I spent on Wallendahl and it was certainly one of the best I have ever had. Bright sunlight beat down on a low river, and there was a good head of sea trout. I fished up from the bottom to the top, taking two-and-a-half hours to do it, and I caught thirteen weighing 30¼ lbs., including two of 6¾ and 7¼ lbs. respectively.

The larger gave me great fun: it eventually took

me down 200 yards where I endeavoured to coax it to a shelving beach. It suddenly dashed between my legs: I executed an acrobatic jump, cursing like an engineer (that I am!), but it would not go where I wanted it. As I struggled there in the shallows, imprecations poured from me, and when I at last netted it (I gave up any idea of beaching), I looked up to see a beautiful Norwegian damsel standing on the high wall above me: she was in fits of laughter. Luckily, so I thought, she won't recognise good, strong, English language. "Congratulations!" she said, "but your swearing was a bit powerful for me!"

Black Pool, round the corner below Wallendahl, is so-called because, for some unaccountable reason, it is one of the few pools to have weed growing on the stones. If the fish are plentiful, it can be excellent with the dry-fly and the sea trout appear to lie over the patches of clean stones among the black ones. It is only about a hundred yards long, and the fisherman progresses some-what uncomfortably up the right bank on rocks and boulders which tend to move whenever your weight is applied — reminiscent of the 'clattering stones' on the approach to a Gaelic fort in the Hebrides.

Salmon often lie in Black Pool. Some years ago, I rose one on a small Jock Scott, half-way down. Next day, I had another cast for it; immediately I had a rise and the fish was hooked. June was beside me, and she played it out over a rather exhausting half-hour on a 9-ft. rod: 15 lbs.

We now come to the Horse Pool. I once asked Malvin "Why 'Horse'?" The rather ridiculous answer came back that, many years ago, a dead horse was found in it!

It is a fascinating pool. It is about one hundred yards long and about sixty yards wide. A wooden platform has been built out from the right bank so that the salmon fishers can cover the water when the river is high in June and July.

But in August, the conditions have changed. Most

of the snow in the mountains has already melted, and the main current has retreated over to the left bank thirty yards away, leaving what we call the 'swimming bath' in between. This water is practically 'dead' and is possibly six or eight feet deep, depending on the height of the river. If you walk along the platform (some six feet above the water surface) you can always discern a number of salmon towards the heavy 'top,' where the stream enters in great volume from the rapids above. Your eye travels downstream to the panorama of sea trout lower down: often there are fish of ten, fifteen or more pounds, lying motionless in the current.

Quite often, in the 'swimming bath' between you and the main stream, an odd salmon or sea trout will be taking a stroll around, slowly gliding through the water as though it were in an aquarium; but, generally speaking, no fish will rise in this part of the pool.

Naturally enough, we do not as a rule walk straight on to the platform. The fish will raise their hats to you and spurn any lure you may like to offer them. If the river is very low, you can wade along on the bottom immediately below the platform with your dry-fly, your back cast just clearing the structure (generally!).

Earlier on, I mentioned Aage Rygh's great triumph in 'Horse' ('Horsh,' he used to call it). He often used an eight foot ladder which he carried across the shallows, and, with its aid, to creep up to the platform level and have a look at the view. He would then insinuate himself horizontally on to the parapet without the risk of being seen by the fish.

Another way of doing it is to crawl on your tummy along the platform from the bank. This method is, as the years go by, progressively irksome. In any case, a large number of protruding nails play havoc with all parts of your dress, and it is a dedicated fisherman who follows this course.

Aagh Rygh was, of course, dedicated. On *his* great

day, he was crawling flat along the wooden platform, preceded by a friend in a similar posture, looking out for the likely fish.

Suddenly the man in front stopped and pointed beneath him: a good salmon or a huge sea trout was lying within ten yards of them. Aage put his dry-fly over it, where it stayed practically motionless. His friend croaked in a hoarse whisper, "It's coming up!" Aage struck, and the fly whistled past his ear. With a Norwegian oath (whatever it was!), he cast the fly again to the same spot — it is extremely unusual for a fish to come again immediately, but where else could he put his fly? "It's coming up again." This time, Aage waited; not till he felt the pull did he tighten.

Then he played the fish: not like most people, including myself, who allow the big fish to play *them*. Running back off the platform and up the bank, he kept a continual strain on the sea trout: side-strain, top-strain, the fish never had a moment's respite. He got it in in nine minutes flat: its head in a net and its tail in his right hand — 24 lbs.! It was at that time considered to be the largest trout ever caught on the dry-fly, and I should think such a record still stands.

The left bank on 'Horse,' beside the stream, can be good for salmon, but for sea trout the tendency for 'drag' is too great, as the fish generally lie on the far side.

Two years ago I was fishing from the platform for salmon. It needed a terrific cast to reach the main stream. I was using a small Hairy Mary, and, half-way down, I hooked a fish. It played magnificently, but we could see it, and realised that the 10/15 pounder was foul-hooked. Very few fish, however large, leave 'Horse,' but this one did. Down into the rapids it went — the wrong side of the rocks. Stumbling, splashing across, I freed the line — then away down again.

Luckily, Andrew was at hand with a gaff, as there was no beach for three hundred yards. I stumbled down under the trees after the fish, and he very dexterously whipped it out as it passed him lower down. It was originally hooked near the base of its ventral fin, but the continual pressure had pulled the hook to within $\frac{1}{8}$" of the tip! Yes — one is sometimes very lucky. It weighed 16 lbs.

The river then flows into a hundred yards of rapids. However, even here, in low water, there are little 'halts' for sea trout between the larger boulders sticking out of the water. One little pool (twenty yards long?) we have called 'Hegg Beg' (a salute to the Gaelic) which often holds a monster waiting for the depth of water, or darkness, to enable him to get up to 'Horse.'

Hegg is, by our results anyway, the best Hauge salmon pool at this time of year: a heavy top, fairly narrow, fining down to Green Bank below. Sea trout can be caught to your salmon rod and possibly mount a Hairy Mary on the left bank as you go up it, and then you change on the way down.

Last year — I can still feel the pang of disappointment — I had caught two grilse on a large yellow fly (it looked ghastly to me) and I was about to stop for lunch when Andrew, sitting high up on the bank opposite, pointed downwards and then stretched his arms wide, indicating a large salmon on the stream below him. In this context I must say that, in our opinion, shouting across even a largish river could alert the fish below. It sets up sound waves which surely can be picked up by the super-sensitive organs of a fish.

So I slowly, diligently worked my way down, casting a long line to the far bank. Just when I judged my fly to be over the fish, I felt a pluck — I pulled in my fly: barb broken on the stones behind me! Will I never learn? I thought. One of the great and ever-absorbing charms of fishing is that one is always learning. In Bridge, I believe the chances of dealing the same hand twice in a lifetime are millions to one against. So in fishing: precise circumstances are seldom, if ever, repeated, but it is a sport in which one first of all tries to master the principles, and for the rest of your life, it is an endeavour to apply these to suit a multitude of specialised circumstances as they arise. But these are so varied that, unless you are a perfect fisherman (and who is?), mistakes will continue to be made. In a life-time's fishing I feel sure that, like Bridge, the same hand will not be dealt to me twice.

Green Bank, immediately below Hegg, must be one of the best sea trout pools in the river (or even in the world). There is a salmon lie on the left bank near the top in high water, but there is at least three hundred yards on both sides of superb dry-fly fishing. Even in the lowest water conditions, it is impossible to cover the centre channel (whence, of course, the big fellows retire if they see too many humans thrashing the water on both sides of them). I have never tried to wade across the pool, except at its extreme foot, but I would say that, at normal river height, the water is in no place more than four to five feet deep. It flows just at that right, slow speed all the way, and to fish up the right bank (the better one), will take you most of the morning. You start at the bottom, and you shouldn't wade deeper than six inches or a foot at the most; in eighteen inches of water you can often spot a four-or a six-pounder's tail slowly waving in the limpid current. The unfortunate tendency is, of course, that the fish (if the stock is not replenished) will gradually sidle into the unreachable channel.

Last year, Andrew caught his big sea trout in Green Bank. For the final hour or so, as it is growing dark, we have a few casts with the wet-fly: Butchers, Peter Ross's, Black Pennells, etc., sizes 8 to 10. I was fishing on the left bank, and Andrew was a hundred yards away on the other side. I was just about to finish — it was practically dark — when I heard the screaming of a reel. There followed a crescendo of sound as he clattered about on the stones, interspersed with shouts and unintelligible

H

mutterings. Apparently he had hooked a large fish which took him several times to the bottom of the pool, a hundred-and-fifty yards below him.

Knut's brother, Olav, was spectating, and Andrew asked him to wade in and try to coax the fish towards the shore. Without demur, he immediately acquiesced, and it was only later, when the battle had ended, that Andrew realised that Olav had no waders on!

The sea trout was finally dragged near the shore, but, by now, it was completely dark, and to try and beach a very large fish in near-complete darkness with a nine-foot rod and 8 lb. B.S. gut, must have posed quite a problem. However, by shortening his line to not more than the length of his rod, he eventually discerned a large, silvery shape at the water's edge.

There was a loud crash and splash as he dropped on the fish as though he were scoring the winning try at Murrayfield, and he stumbled ashore, clutching a 16-pounder to his bosom: a truly magnificent triumph.

We all repaired home and had a couple of drams of Scotch, and when the story had been told and re-told, we wandered outside to look at the night: the dark precipices on either side of the valley against a sky pricked with myriads of pin-points of light, and the eternal soft whisper of that restless river for ever in our ears.

At the bottom of Green Bank, there is a pool which does not belong to us, except for some twenty yards at the top: our beat ceases between the lines of two fences, as shown on the sketch. When the river is low, one can wade out from the right bank and fish the shallow, popply water here: it can be very good. An electric power cable spans the river at this point, hence we call this pocket-handkerchief of water romantically 'Underneath the Pylons.'

We have one further piece of fishing a quarter of a mile further downstream: the lower end of Rock Pool. It is a classic example of the anomalies created by strict riparian ownership. Our piece is wedge-shaped: oblique at the upstream end and straight across at the lower. The Lærdal-Borgund road runs beside, and possibly ten feet, above it. If you walk slowly along — or even crawl forward in the car — every sea trout above a pound weight can be seen hovering on the small yellow stones. You can have a good day on Rock when the fish are running, and when the river is higher, but its great practical advantage is to be able to have a pre-view to see if there are any fish.

This reminds me of the story of the keen fisherman who stopped his car beside a river and started casting in a likely-looking pool. After a certain time, a local wandered along and watched him for a few minutes, and then said:

"Have you caught anything?"

"No — not yet."

"Well — you never will: there aren't any fish in this river."

"Dammit," exploded the fisherman angrily, "why did you have to tell me that? You've completely spoilt my day!"

At the foot of Rock Pool there is, on the right bank, opposite the road, a barrier of huge boulders (probably the remains of an old salmon trap) and the water rushes over these and cascades to a short pool of some fifty yards length — but only the top ten yards are in the Hauge beat. The main stream is generally too heavy for satisfactory dry-fly work, but there are a few yards of quiet water on the near side.

So we have a quarter-of-an-hour's uncomfortable but fascinating stalk at the sea trout which can easily be seen in the comparative calm beside the main current.

As we grow older and find locomotion in a stooping position over an area of dry boulders becomes more irksome, so this particular exercise constitutes an increasing challenge. From the grass, thirty yards away, you can see if there are any fish; if so, then down on your hunkers, slowly inching forward until you are within, say, fifteen yards. I, at that moment, generally collapse uncomfortably to a sitting position on a pile of stones, and start paying out line. Your first cast is right up at the top in the slack water: your fly moves lazily downwards, and just as it is over a fish, the current whips it away downstream. So you try again. If you are lucky, one of the fish will rise, and, when hooked, will rush away as you try and hold it from going down the fifty yards to Hauge Bridge.

I think we all agree that the free-est rising sea trout are those lying in shallow water, such as is so often encountered at the head of a pool, just beside the main current. They have only to tilt backwards from their position to take the fly with the minimum of effort.

I have had a few nice fish from this little patch of water, and Andrew has done ever better. Some years ago, he came out from England with his hand and wrist heavily daubed with gentian-violet, as, two days previously, his stove at home had blown up in his face! (There was black powder in with his coal! but that is a far too complicated story to tell).

He hooked a good fish here, which took him underneath the bridge: he managed to steer it past the nearest pier, and he luckily found a ledge close to his side where he could follow.

The sea trout stopped under the bridge, and he found to his dismay that he could not regain contact as the point of his rod touched the underside of the framework. His injured hand was rubbing along the masonry and blood poured forth. However, eventually the fish proceeded further downstream where he beached it.

We are continually searching out for new sea trout lies. These vary with the height of water, but the really interesting time comes when the river is dead low after a spell of sunny weather. Every little runnel is fished, and it is amazing how often a two- or three-pound sea trout can be picked up in a "pool" of two yards long and in a depth of eight inches. In such circumstances, it is the 'drag' that is the great enemy: so it means down once again on your haunches and a cast of only three or four yards so the line can be lifted off the water before being swept away by the current. It is, of course, nothing like as comfortable as the famous 'down on one knee' attitude of the chalk-stream fisher; in nine cases out of ten, you are crouching on boulders and stones on the Lærdal banks, and a knee-pad can be a very useful adjunct.

In 1962, I unfortunately had to cut short my visit to Lærdal by three or four days, owing to urgent business commitments, and we invited my friend, Nancy Pearson, to fill my place, which she accepted with alacrity. Although not a very experienced fisherwoman, I think she enjoyed her visit, and I know my two companions enjoyed her pany very much.

For her possible benefit, I gave her a description of the beat before she went out, together with a list of general hints and remarks which I feel might interest readers if I include these here, together with some additions suggested by Andrew and Knut.

1. SEA TROUT.

(a) A good eyesight is a great help: some people use Polaroid glasses to advantage. You can then see most of the available fish — but they can also see you if you are within their angle of vision. This fact is another cogent reason why a dry-fly approach from below is preferable in bright sunlight.

(b) Don't clatter about on the stones in hob-nailed waders: wear felt soles, which, in any case, are more sure-footed on weed-free stones. This principle, we feel, could well be applied to most rivers where it is generally impossible to see the fish ("out of sight: out of mind"?)

(c) We nowadays always wear thigh waders exclusively. In the pre-war days, I often used waist waders — I can't think why: possibly because I couldn't afford two pairs! The tendency is always to wade too deep. Aagh Rygh said one day: "Francis, you *walk* on the fish!" — and how right he was. And, incidentally, such a fault is not confined to me or to the Lærdal: it is, in my view, prevalent on nearly every fishing river.

(d) *The strike.* It's not a 'strike': it's a slow tightening: by 'slow,' I mean a full two or three seconds. Towards the end of August there arrives a comparatively thin, muscular type of sea trout, and they require an even longer interval between rise and strike. Incidentally, they play better than any, pound for pound.

One evening last year, on Green Bank, I hooked a sea trout on a No. 8 Peter Ross, and in the first run, it had stripped off a hundred yards of my line. I staggered down after it, and had to shout to Knut as I came upon him (fishing diligently): "Gangway!" I, so tospeak, played through him to the bottom of the pool — at least 200 yards below where I had hooked the fish. It went right to the edge of the rapids, and I asked Knut if he would kindly wade in and try and turn it. I can still see him standing in the river below the sea trout with water slopping over his wader-tops, gently moving upstream with arms outstretched as though he were a shepherd's collie trying to coax six unwilling sheep into a pen!

It worked; and after many sorties, the fish was eventually beached. I walked confidently forward to capture it, when it gave a last flap — and the cast broke! I fell on it in the shallow water, but it wriggled out of my grasp: like a flash, Knut re-entered the river, and, with a majestic heave, threw it high overhead into the long grass behind us. As it was nearly dark, it was a little time before we found it: it was one of these athletic types, having given me twenty minutes of terrific sport, but it only weighed 6¼ lbs.

(e) *Playing the fish.* Concentrate on these words!

So many people allow the fish to play them. When the sea trout is running out, there is not much you can do about it (except to pray that you have enough backing. We cram in 100/120 yards of it, plus 30 yards of line). But when it stops to recuperate its strength — get working. Put strain on from as many different angles as possible: in this way, you will tend to keep it moving. You can also 'walk-up' a sea trout in the same way as you can a salmon.

(f) *Casts.* Nowadays 5 to 8 lb. B.S. nylon. The finest cast is for low water and bright sunlight: the heaviest for wet-fly fishing in the evening.

(g) *Flies: Dry.* I do not think that the full answer has been established in this respect. We have caught them on Tup, Red Palmer, Baigent, Ginger Quill, and many others. These days we use something like our dapping patterns: brown and black or black and white wingless flies, tied on 8 or 10 hooks. As long as it is a perfect floater, you will catch fish: they seldom, if ever, rise to a drowned fly. As far as our experience goes, we feel that the Lærdal sea trout is not the entomological expert that his Test cousin is.

(h) *Line.* It must be heavy enough to facilitate extremely long casting, and light enough not to frighten the fish.

(i) *Rod.* The strongest single-handed trout rod that can be obtained. I use a Farlow 9ft. 6in, which happens to be dubbed the 'Lærdal' rod. The famous Charles Ritz has fished the Lærdal, and I am sure his super parabolic designs would be ideal. The requirement of a rod for dry-fly fishing on the Lærdal is that it will stand up to continuous casting at extreme range in the hand of someone who has a very strong wrist.

2. SALMON.

I am much more diffident in talking about the salmon on Lærdal. I have never fished it at its best

time (June and July): it is one of the most famous
Atlantic salmon rivers in the world. However, in August,
the fish are fewer and, of course, tend to be staler, and
as far as we are concerned, take a back seat as compared
with the sea trout.

However, we like catching the salmon and grilse,
and as we are also very fond of it smoked and "graved! "
so we spend possibly fifteen per cent of our time having
a cast for them.

I do not, therefore, feel qualified to make detailed
suggestions as to rods, flies, etc.: it suffices to say we have
caught salmon on three-inch, deeply sunk monstrosities,
down to size 6 Hairy Marys and other low water patterns.
I have used rods (successfully) from my 14 ft. 6 in.
telegraph pole down to my 9 ft. spare trout rod. If we
become impatient, we hurl some kind of ironmongery into
Horse Pool to achieve our salmon quota and then quickly
turn all our attention to our sporting favourite, the sea
trout!

3. GENERAL REMARKS.

(1) We fish for pleasure, not as a business. There
are those who fish the Lærdal and a lot of other rivers
as though it were a commercial operation. A shift system
is followed, and the whole object is to get the fish (generally
salmon) out of the water by any means, short of netting
the pools.

This tendency is, of course, understandable: over the
past decade or two, the price demanded for fishing beats
has soared, and the only way it can be afforded by the
average sportsman, is by selling the catch. It would be
much better for the sport generally if the value of salmon
on the market were 20 or 30p per pound instead of
over £1.

(2) Always think of the farmer when crossing his
fields to the river: this, of course, applies to all rivers
in all countries. Do not walk through growing crops: this

sounds obvious, but I have often seen fishermen walking straight across a standing hayfield.

Use gates wherever possible: continual climbing of fences ultimately ruins them.

(3) As I have already explained elsewhere, the fishing in Norway belongs to the riparian farmers. When we on occasion have more fish than we require either for immediate consumption or for store in the deep-freeze for taking back to the U.K., we distribute such surplus to our local hosts and their friends and relations in the hamlet. The goodwill and comradeship thus engendered is worth far more than the few odd pounds we would get if we sold it.

(4) When we are on the river, we certainly fish hard. However, on occasion, when the water is abnormally low and the fish are few and far between, we take a day's — or half a day's — rest. Last year, we hired a taxi and went over the new road to Aurland. It was a delightful trip, and next day we returned to our river refreshed.

To derive the greatest enjoyment from our sport, it is essential that it never becomes a duty. The spread of competitive fishing is, in our view, a sad trend. We spend most of our lives in a highly competitive society, and to relax from this arduous existence for a few weeks in a year, constitutes the perfect holiday. It is an attitude of mind well worth cultivating, and I think we three at Lærdal have the right approach in that, although each naturally longing for the best sport possible, competition, as such, does not exist, and we all get a great kick out of each other's triumphs as well as out of our own.

We have followed a custom since the war of giving a little cocktail party for our hosts at Hauge. The doyen of the district is Mr Lasse Hauge, Anne Sofie's uncle. The party consists of possibly eight or ten guests, and it seems not to matter one jot if Knut is the only one present who is fully conversant with both languages! A year or two ago, I had the temerity to tell a funny story to our

Norwegian friends by means of extravagant gesticulations and blood-curdling grimaces. They laughed till the tears ran down their cheeks, but I rather fancy it was not the joke that was responsible (they could not possibly have understood it): it was, rather, the sight of a Scotsman making a fool of himself.

Every year we receive an invitation to visit Mr and Mrs Lasse Hauge in their house, where we eat home-made cakes and drink liqueurs and listen to the gramophone playing the fantastic Hardanger Fiddle, practically a one-man band on strings!

Lærdal to us has become part of our life. The country and the people and the fishing and the warm friendship within our own party add up to a sum of happiness beyond the reach of any alternative. Andrew starts crossing off the weeks around April for our August fishing! This I think is overdoing it: he is pressing Time — it goes too fast anyway. The knowledge that *tempus fugit* should make us sit back and enjoy the panorama of our fleeting life — like a passenger in a train happily viewing the passing countryside with infinite patience, but, with mounting excitement, awaiting the arrival of a place called Lærdal!

Twilight of a Fisherman

I sweep between the sheets and my feet search out the cool corners of the bed. Lærdal in a fortnight! I smile and, as my thoughts meander down the misty corridors of memory and anticipation, they flit to and fro over the river valley of my dreams.

I am poised a few feet above the gliding stream at Wallendahl. My fly is propelled a hundred yards to the choppy water cascading down from the neck. A huge, boiling rise . . . a heavy pull downstream . . .

The fish is on the stones — looks like a large plaice as it flaps until despatched. A sea trout — a big sea trout: how to get it to the car?

I am waiting for the Morris Traveller: the fish lies in the deep grass. June arrives — "any luck?" she asks. I point. "Gosh . . . ! How? When? Where?"

I arrive back at the house. Andrew and Knut are there already. I raise the fish out of the back of the car and flop it on to the table. "Good Lord! How big?" We hoist it on to the spring-balance: 18 pounds. "Must go down to the butcher's and find out its exact weight," says Knut. Our host, hostess and their three charming daughters crowd in. Stella, the Alsatian, lopes around, barking in excitement. The grey-striped kitten nuzzles the fish's head as it lies there — inert and huge.

In the butcher's: verdict — 8 kilos: $8 \times 2 = 16 + 10\% = 17.6 = 17$ lbs. 10 ozs.

Elation and tiredness and contentment and sleep drive me onwards through mists of sunshine and shadow and increasing worldlessness.

I sit in the deep shade under the trees beside Hegg. I gaze out over the fifty yards of sun-drenched boulders to myself — casting a long line over the salmon lie. He is young. Yes — he is very young. With a momentary pang of realisation, I take his place. I cast; I hook something heavy and immoveable. Slowly the unyielding weight bears downstream. I step on a rock which capsizes — I am in the water. My waders fill and I am beneath the surface, floating down . . . down . . . down . . . dark, cavernous boulders and pale green, watery surface-light alternate in my fading vision as I slowly turn over and over.

"Famous fisherman drowned in Norway: fifty-pound salmon still attached to line." "A perfect bore: couldn't fish — always pretended he could . . .".

I chuckle in the limbo between consciousness and sleep: my face on the pillow is cast in stone on the way to oblivion. I sway downwards, memory glimpses flashing across my transient vision . . . dark fog and dreaminess: a blur of valley and river and greenness and happy faces and dust roads and the glory of companionship.

An early morning breeze wafts the mists upstream: I float with them over the Rock Pool, around the corner and high over Green Bank. The placid, clear water flows over sand-coloured stones: the fish look like miniature tadpoles gently undulating in apparent atmosphere. I sweep skywards in an upsurge of air current and view the valley beneath: the green potato fields and apple orchards: the red and multi-coloured houses nestling in their cushion: the blue, meandering river twinkling to right and to left: the road ribboned down the valley . . . up and up I soar: the vertical precipices sweep past . . . sparkling waterfalls gushing and tumbling . . . Up . . . up — and then to the open space of the Universe: the Jotunheim prick their dazzling white summits to the blue . . . I heave a big sigh of utter contentment in my dream. My body lies limp and unconscious in my bed. My soul is beyond . . . in sleep . . .

CHAPTER 9

LAST CAST

And so I come to my last cast: it is always a nostalgic moment for all fishermen when this arrives. I have read over my Fishing Diary covering more than forty years and have tried to select memories which I feel would interest others, some possibly who are not necessarily ardent fishermen. I suppose when one is relaxing from the daily toils of professional life, the happiness enjoyed is not solely derived from the pastime itself. Where my sport is concerned, the central theme must also include the background experience in the same way that the decoration of a beautiful home is as important as the house itself.

It may seem, reading through these pages, that my friends and I do nothing else on our holiday than catch large baskets of salmon and trout. Of course, I have picked out the better days to describe, and, to cut myself down to size, I would like to quote some figures *The Field* published recently. Here they are:

1. Total days fished: 838.

2. Total number of salmon and trout killed: 2738.

3. As I frequently walk 10 miles per day to distant hills and lochs (I once fished down 10 miles of the Don with the wet-fly in one day for 10 trout: how inefficient I must have been!), I would hazard a conservative estimate as to the distance walked at four miles per day; so, altogether (say, approximately the distance from London to New York!): 3352 miles.

4. This means about one fish per one and a quarter miles.

5. I should guess that, out of the average fishing day of eight hours, I may be casting for four hours. As

average time per cast may be 12 seconds, total casts would be, per day: 1200.

6. Therefore, total costs made in 40 years: 1,005,600. (What! Over a million casts? It makes my arm tired to think of it!)

7. Therefore, number of casts per fish: 370. (As depressing as that?)

8. And, lastly, the average cast might be 15 yards, so the distance covered by my flies might be 15 yards drawing in: say, 50 yards per cast. (This is conservative, as I almost invariably 'false-cast').

I now arrive at the horrifying figure from (7) above that my flies have travelled about 28,000 miles, and that a sizeable fish is hooked, landed and knocked on the head every 10.4 miles of fly-travel!

The only sane conclusion that can be reached by man or computer is that fishing is, at best, a sport of the fanatic, or just of the purely unbalanced.

And now I come to the end; I feel I cannot do better than to quote—as my father did in his book *I Go A-fishing* —my kinsman's, Andrew Lang's poem, written over half a century ago:

> *Within the streams, Pausanias saith,*
> *That down Cocytus valley flow,*
> *Girdling the grey domain of Death,*
> *The spectral fishes come and go;*
> *The ghosts of trout flit to and fro.*
> *Persephone, fulfil my wish;*
> *And grant that in the shades below*
> *My ghost may land the ghosts of fish.*

Yes, indeed! And may you share this glorious Fate with me!